# Beyond Heartache

## Margaret Johnson

KINGSWAY PUBLICATIONS

EASTBOURNE

ISBN 0 86065 098 7

TO CINDY . . .
*My daughter . . .*
*My friend . . .*

Printed in Great Britain for
KINGSWAY PUBLICATIONS LTD
Lottbridge Drove, Eastbourne, E. Sussex BN23 6NT by
Richard Clay (The Chaucer Press) Ltd, Bungay, Suffolk

# Contents

## ACKNOWLEDGMENTS

This book was written with the help of many fellow-sufferers along the Heartache Road. I am deeply grateful for each one who was willing to share his or her story, even though it meant reliving unhappy times and remembering grievous days. Some of the names and places have been altered to protect the privacy of those who wished to remain anonymous.

My thanks to Bob DeVries of Zondervan who first encouraged me to write this book and to Judy Markham, my friend and editor, who reassured me along the way and with her expertise brought the manuscript together into a readable book.

And always . . . my deepest "thank you" to my husband, Vern, for his patience, support, and unselfishness in allowing me time and space to think, to write and rewrite.

# Preface

I do not believe God had anything to do with your daughter's death. It was Satan who caused it."

Struggling to keep my face from registering shocked amazement, I listened to these words from a woman acquaintance paying a condolence visit a few days after our eighteen-year-old daughter's fatal accident. I was shocked that she supposed her matter-of-fact statement would be a comfort. And I was amazed that my reaction was so physically intense in spite of my state of numb disbelief following Kathi's death.

My visitor sat quietly, pious in her certainty that a loving God did not allow tragedy, hinting that He was

5

impotent against the strategies of Satan.

At least that is what *I* heard her say.

My outraged heart was too filled with fresh grief to respond with words lest they tumble out and angry tears fall with them. Only days had passed since the accident which had claimed the lives of three teen-agers, including our daughter Kathi. I was still in shock, refusing to believe she was gone.

My husband, Vern, had made quiet but necessary arrangements while family and friends flowed through our home offering love and comfort. During those days my thoughts were constantly scrambling for half-forgotten promises from God's Word. The sand of grief was deep and shifting; I needed solid ground —absolute assurance that God had not slipped or made a careless mistake.

And then slowly I remembered the wonderful promises of God to His children. Rivers of peace stilled my restless heart into blessed quietness.

"My times are in your hands" (Ps. 31:15).

"All the days ordained for me were written in your book before one of them came to be" (Ps. 139:16).

"It is *appointed* for men to die once" (Heb. 9:27 NASB).

*"The Lord gave and the Lord has taken away"* (Job 1:21).

I clung to those promises like a blind person in a strange place, and when unanswered "whys" wrenched my heart, those assurances became an anchor. Kathi had met her divine appointment! Her work on earth was done. God had known all along, even when she was still in my womb, that He had ordained for her the brief span of eighteen years plus six months.

For reasons known only to Him, the *Lord* had given Kathi and the *Lord* had taken her away. In His own time. In His own way.

6

Faith was a friend during heartsick days.

Yet when I drove by Kathi's school on a rainy afternoon I remembered other rainy days when she had phoned for me to pick her up by the flagpole; or a song of the sixties flowing from the stereo would melt my strong resolve into misty tears.

On those grief-filled days, all the faith in the world could not dry my tears. It was difficult to concede, but often they were tears of rage at God who let her die, tears of anger at the curving highway that claimed her life, and even tears of resentment toward Kathi for leaving.

Suffering is not always logical!

During the first holidays following her death, my depression deepened. One time I actually picked out a blouse as a Christmas gift for Kathi and in a sudden shock of remembrance laid it back on the counter. I rushed from the store in tears.

Christmas was painful. I remember standing by the dining room table helplessly trying to set the usual buffet, holding eight plates in my arms and unable to think where to place them. A tear escaped, and others quickly followed.

I felt an arm encircle my waist. It was Cindy, our oldest daughter. "Mom," she said tenderly, taking one plate away, "we only need seven plates this year."

"I know." I was sobbing. "I forgot."

"Look at it this way, mom," Cindy comforted. "There are seven empty places in heaven waiting for us. We're on our way, but Kathi is *Home*."

My mind said yes; me heart screamed no. I longed to touch and hold Kathi once more, to stop my nightly dreams where she was running through the house flashing her wide engaging smile and calling "See you later."

7

Birthdays in our home are celebrated with a festive family dinner, and when I turned the calendar on that March morning it was so painful to see her birth date in print that I quickly turned the page.

Objects stumbled on in odd moments joined relentlessly to push me further along the suffering road: third-class mail addressed to Kathi; an old blouse at the back of a drawer; a fragment of poetry in her clear handwriting; a hurried note addressed to me on the back of her music book.

Then I wrote a book which told Kathi's story. The writing brought surprisingly therapeutic release, washing my face with cleansing tears as I walked back through her life dredging up memories that must be faced and resolved.

With the publication of *18 . . . No Time to Waste,* a flood of letters and telephone calls from bereaved parents beseeched, "Can you help us? Can we talk to you?" The grief was always the same; only the faces were different. And as I held cold hands, offered Kleenex, listened, nodded, prayed, wept, my own suffering became diminished and, quite to my joyous surprise, I was ready to reenter the world and make something creative from my loss.

Looking back, I clearly see that reaching out to other bereaved parents was the beginning of my own healing.

I remember Janice! We sat together one hot July afternoon as she told her story in fragmented sentences.

"Jeff was in college . . . ready to come home for the holidays . . . packing, when . . . when . . . a fire broke out in the dorm. All the boys got out, but Jeff . . . Jeff went back for his guitar . . . his *guitar.*" She put her hand to her eyes. In my imagination I could envision a husky blond boy racing up wooden stairs to his room to search for his guitar, unaware that flames were close and threatening.

"You've done so well since Kathi's death," Janice sobbed. "What's wrong with me?"

I touched her arm. "Janice, I'm further along the road, that's all."

There seemed to be no end to tragedy now that I had tasted it. Had I been so oblivious to the deaths of young people, or were they dying in greater numbers than before? Everywhere I turned there was a bereaved parent aching for comfort. And I had learned from my own heartache that the best gift I could offer was a listening heart.

Not a string of quoted Scripture verses. That could come later.

Not a lecture about God's will. I didn't know His will for them.

Not an elusive reference to their loved ones. The subject could not be avoided.

The bereaved wished to remember and to share their memories. Some of my own greatest joys had been letters and calls from Kathi's friends who shared their own memories of her.

"I saw Kathi just last month (or last week) and we had a great time."

"I met Kathi on the beach just the week before the accident, and she was so excited about going to that camp."

I devoured these conversations, listening as though it were news from a far country.

Now I could do the same for others!

One month before Kathi's death we had received word from my hometown that friends had lost their three-year-old son in a drowning accident. I knew how special their little boy was to them; they had been married twenty years before he was born—a unique gift, so wanted, so adored. But at the time I had no way of evaluating their grief. I signed the sympathy card, "You are in our prayers."

A month later when we lost Kathi, my friend, the little boy's mother, sent a long condolence letter. Now we could communicate with mutual understanding.

Comfort has far greater meaning when it comes from another's own personal experience of grief.

As time passed, I was often asked to speak and share Kathi's story. Through this outreach, I became acquainted with many other hurting people. While their circumstances varied, they all shared similar human responses of grieving, of suffering and asking "why." I realized that if my sharing about my own heartache could comfort or encourage bereaved parents, then perhaps somehow sharing these other forms of heartache could comfort those in like circumstances. The ideal way to do this seemed to be to tell some of these stories in a book.

In preparing this book, I was amazed that so many were waiting to pour out their hurts, for every story in these pages is true. I have chosen carefully, desiring that the overcoming lives of others who have walked through deep valleys would be universally helpful in reaching those who are traveling along the road of suffering and heartache.

You may wish to read this book in intervals, for each chapter is complete in itself. Some stories may touch your particular hurt, and hopefully the knowledge that you are not alone in your valley may soften your grief.

As you enter into the lives of the people in these pages, you will discover that they have found a place beyond heartache, a welcome haven after the dark. The path along the way had many stops and starts, went through deep valleys, and was surrounded by high mountains, but somewhere, sometime, acceptance was embraced and quite unexpectedly, often with joyful surprise, they were on their way to restoration.

It is my prayer that this will be a book of hope and that you will find, as have millions of other sufferers on the heartache road, the One who promised to give "Beauty for ashes; joy instead of mourning; praise instead of heaviness" (Isa. 61:3 LB).

*"For I know the plans I have for you, says the Lord. They are plans for good and not for evil, to give you a future and a hope."*

*Jeremiah 29:11 LB*

Before
I Sleep

# 1  Before I Sleep

It was a beautiful spring day. The sky was blue and cloudless, a perfect setting for the brilliance of white and fuchsia lilacs budding on softly bending branches in the morning breeze.

Kathi was five, and Vern and I were driving her to the hospital for a tonsillectomy. I wondered with a touch of anxiety how it would be possible to leave my little girl with strangers in a busy hospital ward knowing how she disliked being away from home overnight. We had gone through the hospital procedure carefully with the help of a children's book, *My Visit to the Hospital*, and she had anticipated a fun adventure until now. I could see that her dark eyes were wide with apprehension.

We signed for Kathi's room and followed the floor nurse as she walked briskly along green-tiled corridors through the children's ward. Kathi clutched her teddy bear, looking around anxiously at the sights and sounds of suffering children: infants crying in wailing disharmony, babies surrounded by i.v. bottles taped to their arms, and young children walking listlessly through the halls, robes wrapped loosely about them. Vern carried Kathi the last short distance to her room.

Kathi's roommate was a frail girl, too small for her three years, lying in a crib surrounded by hospital paraphernalia. She turned her head when we tiptoed in, but no interest sparked in her dark-circled eyes. Kathi laid her head on Vern's shoulder, her small arm wrapped tightly around his neck.

"It's okay, honey," he assured her softly. We made a game of tying her new pink robe around her, slipping on her bunny slippers, and walking down the hall to the play area where children in wheelchairs were gazing indifferently at the black and white television perched on a shelf. Kathi didn't move from her spot on Vern's lap.

When we knew it was time to leave, we took Kathi back to her room and elaborately tucked her into bed, placing her teddy bear in her arms. I swallowed the rising sensation of tears and leaned over to kiss her gently. As I did, my eyes caught a glimpse of the next room which was petitioned off by glass.

I straightened! In that room were two little girls, identical twins, and sitting between their beds was a young woman, obviously in her last months of pregnancy. She sat perfectly still, a tender look of pain-filled love softening her face. One twin was inert, lying on her side, her curly hair dampened with fever while the other one appeared healthy as any three-year-old, bouncing in the crib cluttered with books and toys.

Kathi's eyes followed my gaze.

"What's wrong with them, mommy? Are they having their tonsils out, too?"

"I don't know, honey." I kissed her good-night once more. "Daddy and I have to leave now, but I'll be here first thing in the morning."

She turned on her side clutching her fuzzy toy animal, trying to keep the tears from falling.

Vern and I walked back through the hall, a prayer of gratitude spilling from my heart for our two healthy girls and a much-wanted, year-old son.

I asked the nurse at the station, "The twins next to our daughter—what—?"

"Leukemia," she said softly. "One is nearly gone."

"Oh," I glanced back down the hall. "How can that mother stand knowing—"

The nurse stopped writing in her ledger and looked directly at me. "I've been nursing for twenty years, and that situation is as heartbreaking as anything I have seen. The parents come each day never knowing which one will be the last for their girls. They've been so sweetly courageous. It must be their strong religious faith."

We had a deep faith in God, Vern and I, a personal relationship with Jesus Christ. But to lose a child—two children—would our faith carry us through such grief?

I was very much aware of the sting of death. That unwelcome intruder had snatched away three close friends and my brother before I turned seventeen. I knew the empty feeling of losing someone close, but I shut my eyes tight against gathering tears imagining the hurt of losing one of my children. It was unthinkable!

The following morning I was at the hospital and in Kathi's room before she returned from surgery. In the next room the husband was there beside his wife, tenderly holding the twin who had been playing so happily the night before. Now she was fitful, resting her head on her daddy's shoulder, whimpering through swollen lips. The other child lay in the same inert position, her head thrown back, hair damp and curly around her fragile face.

Throughout the day as Kathi recuperated I applied cool cloths to her face and held cracked ice to her parched mouth. In the evening I spoon-fed ice cream while she awakened and slept fitfully.

But it was the glass-petitioned room that held my attention; before my eyes a drama was taking place, and I was the witness to sustained courage in spite of heartbreak.

Thursday, three days after surgery, Kathi could come home. When Vern and I arrived, she was sitting up in bed patiently waiting, her coloring books held in her arms, her pink robe buttoned lopsidedly. I laughingly rebuttoned her robe trying to keep my eyes from straying to the room next door. But it was impossible! I felt my insides churn. Only one child lay there now, tubes strapped to a bruised arm. The other bed was empty. The pregnant mother sat erectly beside her daughter, her face a prayer. I sensed that the absent twin was dead and that this one was in the final stages of dying.

Just once the woman looked up, and our eyes met, one mother to another. Her eyes were acquainted with a grief I could not fathom. I wanted to smile but quickly closed my lips against it. Would it be right to smile at such a time? But in that suspended moment I saw a faint curve of her lips, and she nodded slightly as though to say it *was* all right. She needed my smile.

My husband and I walked beside Kathi's wheelchair which was pushed by an aid who chatted to her young charge. And Kathi, sore throat and all, was chatting back. Happy. She was going home.

Children's ward was a memory that did not quickly fade. Now I was aware that only miles away from our home there was a world of suffering. Especially I would not forget the twins, and I wondered often about the little girls and their loving parents.

One evening, months later, I opened the newspaper and there were the twins' smiling faces, photographed during healthier days. An interview with the mother told about their battle with leukemia, a battle they had lost. Though many years have passed still I remember some of the answers that young mother gave the inquiring reporter:

"God has given us a little boy, and we are so happy, but nothing or no one can ever take our daughters' place. We know they are with Jesus and are no longer suffering, and that is our comfort. When we first saw those ugly bruises on one twin, we could scarcely believe the doctor's verdict of leukemia. And when weeks later I was bathing the other twin and saw the same bluish bruises on her legs, my hands began to shake. It was the lowest moment of my life. I knew I had to be strong, but by myself it was impossible. God gave my husband and I strength we never would have dreamed possible; even measures of joy that we have locked in our memory forever—of holding our girls close before they died and releasing them to their heavenly Father."

I recall thinking, "*I'm a Christian, too. I have faith. Could*

*I feel that way if I lost a child? Would I?"* I measured my faith and found it wanting. I didn't think I could. I folded the newspaper and looked up at the summer sky. In the twilight stars were beginning to twinkle, and the faint outline of the moon rested between the trees. *"Lord, I couldn't. Don't ask me to give up any of my children."*

Kathi grew to be an adolescent, a vivacious teen-ager. And though I didn't actually watch her die, I *did* have to travel that road after all. One I would not have dreamed I could travel that summer evening thirteen years before.

During the dark September days after the shock of Kathi's death, I remembered watching those parents and the silent testimony that had been recorded on my memory. It was then I understood that *God gives grace for the moment of need.*

Three Septembers after Kathi's death I was once again attending a funeral. That day the usual oppressive heat and thick smog settled uncomfortably in the San Fernando Valley shrouding the mountains from view, and as I walked with friends toward the church, I swallowed hard against the lump in my throat. The coffin stood on the very spot where Kathi's had been. The church was packed with people paying their final respects to the wife of a leading community member. It was the funeral of my friend, Jeanie.

Our pastor eulogized Jeanie, but I scarcely heard. My thoughts were racing back to the previous September when I first met her. . . .


## Jeanie

I was lying in our backyard on the lounge enjoying the later afternoon sunshine after a busy day of speaking at a luncheon. There was just enough time for a short rest in the sunshine before preparing dinner, and I was relishing the solitude when the telephone rang. I was tempted to ignore it, but the caller was persistent so I arose reluctantly to answer. That was my first encounter with Jeanie Wilson.

"This is Jeanie Wilson. My daughter Beth graduated with Kathi," she introduced herself. "I've read your book about Kathi, and I was wondering—could I come and visit you, say tomorrow?"

The call surprised me. Beth had told me about her parents' antagonism to her new faith in Christ, their refusal to read Kathi's story, their dislike of anything religious.

"Why—why yes, I'd like that, Jeanie," I said quickly. When she said good-by, I wondered, Why the urgency to see me tomorrow? Why did she sound so troubled? Is she angry with me for spending time with Beth? Is she coming to warn me not to see her daughter again?

Jeanie was at my door promptly at ten in the morning, a colorful scarf covering her head. I poured cups of tea, served slices of banana bread, and listened to Jeanie as she began to explain:

"I'm recovering from brain surgery," she said, "hence the scarf." She laughed quickly, and I wondered whether to join her or express sympathy. I did neither.

"I came to tell you, Margaret," she touched my hand briefly, "that I have found peace and freedom from fear through reading Kathi's story. You see, before I knew I had a brain tumor I read your book, thinking at the time it was sweet that Kathi had such a strong faith, but not feeling that we, Bill and I, needed anything. As for Beth, we felt she was over-reacting to her friend's death. Kind of a dramatic gesture. Religion has not been a part of our life, you see.

21

"Until—until the doctor diagnosed my blacking-out spells and headaches as a brain tumor with the prognosis of terminal cancer. He told us that I have only one year to live. Well—we did need faith in a hurry.

"It was while I was on the stretcher being wheeled to the operating room that I prayed for the first time in years. I said, 'God, if You will let me live through this operation, I will go home and learn about You and help my family find You too.' I made a promise, a promise I mean to keep. I remembered the Robert Frost lines about 'promises to keep, and miles to go before I sleep.' That's the way I feel. I have much, so much to do in my one year.

"I asked God to make Himself real to me, and He did. When I awakened after that surgery, I knew He was giving me time. Time to learn. I wonder—maybe you could help me study the Bible and understand more about God. I am so primary," she laughed in a shaken voice. "All I really know is that my sins are forgiven through Jesus Christ."

I assured Jeanie I would be happy to study the Bible with her.

Jeanie was a quick student, calling a number of times a day with a flood of questions. We spent hours over God's Word, praying, weeping, trying to hold back the year. Jeanie was in a race against time.

One day she came to my door clutching the Sunday paper, a pressing question on her mind.

"Margaret, what does this word 'rapture' mean?" She pointed to our pastor's Sunday sermon which was printed in the *Los Angeles Times*.

I led her to our family room and reached for a contemporary paraphrase of the Bible so she could clearly understand.

22

Jeanie read aloud:

> And now, dear brothers, I want you to know what
> happens to a Christian when he dies so that when it
> happens you will not be full of sorrow, as those who
> have no hope. For since we believe that Jesus died and
> then came back to life again, we can also believe that
> when Jesus returns, God will bring back with him all the
> Christians who have died.
>
> I can tell you this directly from the Lord: that we who are
> still living when the Lord returns will not rise to meet him
> ahead of those who are in their graves. For the Lord
> himself will come down from heaven with a mighty shout
> and with the soul-stirring cry of the archangel and the
> great trumpet-call of God. And the believers who are
> dead will be the first to rise to meet the Lord. Then we
> who are still alive and remain on the earth will be caught
> up (raptured) with them in the clouds to meet the Lord in
> the air and remain with him forever (2 Thess. 4:13-17
> LB, italics mine).

"Then maybe," Jeanie's face brightened, "maybe
it could happen before—" Unspoken words lay
between us.

After Christmas, Jeanie called, weeping into the
telephone.

"Margaret," she sobbed, "no one has to tell me. I know.
Another tumor is growing."

"Oh, Jeanie," I said, "I'm so sorry."

"I'm all right, really I am, but this is so unfair to Bill and
the children."

Once more Jeanie had surgery and the offending
growth was removed. I went to visit her in a flower-filled
room, cards everywhere, tributes to a much-loved
woman. She was smiling.

"You won't believe this!" she said. "But I think I'm

23

cured—yes, I'm sure of it. Oh, praise the Lord, I'm not going to die after all!"

My heart lifted with a faint ray of hope. Perhaps she *was* healed this time. But one look at the doctor's ominously closed face told another story.

Jeanie insisted on having bright, colorful posters in her room. One read, "God does not love you if . . . He loves you period."

The little booklet, *Faith is . . .*, had gone into surgery with her, and now the memorized pages lay torn on her bedstand.

One day she phoned from the hospital excited over a new discovery.

"Margaret," she exclaimed, "I've just found the secret to living the Christian life. I was leafing through my Bible and discovered a verse that will take care of all problems, anxieties, quarrels. Listen—" And she began to read familiar words from David's nineteenth psalm. "Let the words of my mouth, and the meditation of my heart, be acceptable in thy sight, O Lord, my strength, and my redeemer."

"Isn't that beautiful?" Her voice was smiling; the childlikeness of her faith brought tears to my eyes.

"Yes, it is, Jeanie," I whispered.

When she came home, she was eager to get on with her studies, to learn, to grow. Her energy exceeded mine, and I wanted to say, "Hey, Jeanie, slow down," but it would have been like asking the sun to stop shining.

Jeanie was remembering her promise and traveling the last miles full of excitement and faith. Each time there was a service at the church, Jeanie and her husband were there. She took notes furiously as though, in spite of her insistence that she was healed, she knew deep inside that she only had a mile to go.

24

One warm April evening Bill phoned. "Jeanie's going in for surgery Friday. They've found another tumor."

We joined the family in the waiting room the night before her third and last operation. I was amazed at Jeanie's light spirit and infectious laughter. When her surgeon stopped by briefly, she quipped, "It's a rather expensive way to get a haircut, don't you think?"

"That's not funny," he said abruptly.

But Jeanie was keeping it light for her family. Serious thoughts were written in a letter for her doctor if she didn't make it through the operation. After her mother's death, Beth showed me Jeanie's letter.

*Dear Dr. Raymond,*

*If you are reading this letter, I will be gone. Please don't think in any way that you have failed. If I do not come through, then it is God's perfect will for me to go be with Him. Thank you for all you have done.*

This time Jeanie's recovery was slower and more painful. Bill ushered me into intensive care where she lay, her face as white as the bandage around her head.

I held her ice-cold hand. "Jeanie," I whispered, "I love you." I didn't think she could hear me, but her lips moved. "I know you do, Margaret. I know." I expected those to be her last words to me; she was in great pain and so cold. But within a week Jeanie was home, the scarf once again covering her shorn hair.

One night late in the summer Vern and I invited Bill and Jeanie to our home for the evening. I was refilling her cup with coffee when Jeanie spoke unforgettable words.

"You know, the first thing I am going to do when I get to heaven, after I thank the Lord for His great salvation, will be to say, 'Thank you, Kathi, for leading the way to Jesus.'"

A hand squeezed my heart for I sensed that Jeanie had finally embraced acceptance and knew she was going to die. Her year was nearly up, and this was her way of saying good-by, and "thank you" for the past months.

But it was really Jeanie who had taught *me*; it had been *her* faith, *her* courage, *her* strength in the face of death. I had been the student in life's darkest classroom. She had given me a legacy of hope in the face of hopelessness, of trust in the sureness of God's promises.

I spent an afternoon with Jeanie by her pool one hot August afternoon, and as we talked she shared her deepest thoughts. Her ten-year-old daughter, Sandy, was splashing with friends in the shallow end of the pool.

"It's my children—it's leaving them that hurts the most. Sandy is so young. I don't want to leave her . . . I hope Bill marries soon . . . I've had a good life."

Jeanie was saying good-by to life, to all she knew and loved. She was on her last mile.

I only saw her once more. Vern and I went to their home one evening to say good-by before Bill and Jeanie left on a short anniversary trip to San Francisco.

"We were married there," Jeanie explained. Bill and the doctor had consented after her insistence that she was well enough to make the trip. It was something she wanted to do.

We stood in their driveway on that summer evening and said the usual things you say to someone you love when you think you will see them soon.

"Have a wonderful time," I called through the car window as we left, and she waved, smiling widely.

Bill and Jeanie had their week in San Francisco, but at the end she was flown home desperately ill, rushed to intensive care in excruciating pain that the heaviest medication could not relieve.

26

This time the tumor was inoperable. I wanted so badly to tiptoe to her side, hold her cold hand, and whisper again, "I love you, Jeanie," but I could not. So I replayed the words from the last time when she had assured me, "I know you do, Margaret. I know."

Beth called early one morning and said quietly, "Mrs. Johnson, my mom's with the Lord. She died last night."

Death had marched through the corridors of my life in swift succession the past five years touching our immediate family—first my father, then our daughter, next my oldest brother, and finally my adopted sister. Now mourning bells were ringing for a dear friend, whose cheery voice I would never hear again this side of heaven.

The past five years had been heavy with sorrow. It seemed sometimes there could be no tears left, but that morning I wept once more for Jeanie. She had hurried through my life for one brief year, but that year had pushed us into a closeness that under normal circumstances would have taken years to develop.

Sometimes even grief is a gift. It had brought Bill and Jeanie to the foot of the cross.

At the funeral home where friends gathered to visit and pray with Bill, his voice broke with tears when he spoke. "I've had such peace, such comfort through this, and it's all because of Jesus."

A fresh wind of joy flowed through my mind with the remembered words of hope.

> *Death has been swallowed up in victory.*
> *Where, O death, is your victory?*
> *Where, O death, is your sting?*
> *The sting of death is sin, and the power of sin is the law.*
> *But thanks be to God! He gives us the victory through our Lord Jesus Christ (1 Cor. 15:54-56).*

Going
Home

# 2  Going Home

I t was a warm May day, a lazy Saturday afternoon, the kind of day that wraps itself around you with luxuriant arms after the house is shining clean and the children are out playing. I lay on the sofa absorbed in the quiet, dividing my attention between the book I was reading and the beauty of the flowering myrtle tree outside the window.

In the background, music was playing softly and beyond that I could faintly hear my husband talking in low tones on the telephone. When I couldn't catch his phrases, I closed my eyes relishing my delightful afternoon intermission.

Vern walked into the living room, sat down beside me, and took my hand. "Honey," he said, "that was your mother. She wanted me to tell you—your father has leukemia."

And just like that my tranquillity was shattered. The melodious sounds from the stereo were suddenly annoying. I sat up quickly. Leukemia spelled only one thing to me—DEATH.

"Oh, no—how—how long does he have?"

"The doctor couldn't say." Vern held me close, warming my suddenly chilled body. "Your mother doesn't want him to know. She wants us to let him enjoy these last months, so we mustn't let on anything is wrong."

"Oh, I couldn't do that. He's ready to go. He would want to know."

Vern hushed my tears, cradling me tenderly while I sat in the first throes of grief. My father was already two years over the allotted seventy. Wasn't that a good age? But this was *my* father, *my* life, *my* pillar that would be gone, and it was *my* grief that was cutting edges around my heart.

The next day was Mother's Day, and we went to my parents' home for dinner, lingering at the table for conversation and dessert. No one looking in could have guessed that death was waiting in the shadows. How do you hide the sure knowledge that the person across from you is dying? And how can you hide the tears from your eyes, your voice? How can you refrain from touching his hand and pleading, "I love you. Please don't go."

"You're just like your dad," everyone had always said. It was true. We were alike. We understood each other, felt the same emotions, loved the same things—books and writings and words. He had invested a lifetime of diligent

32

study in the Bible, and I was his most avid listener.

I remembered something dad said once. "Margaret, I've asked the Lord to allow all my family to gather around when I die just like Jacob (how he related everything in his life to Scripture!) so that I can say good-bye to those I love."

Now I felt sure his desire would be granted.

The following week when I telephoned my parents, I sensed my father's spirits were failing along with his health.

After our usual greeting, he said, "Do you want to talk to your mother?"

"No," I said, berating myself for the years I had not called simply to talk to him. "I've just called to chat with you."

He began talking about the past, of his mistakes and failures, real or imagined. I assured him that, no, he had not failed, he had done the best he could, and more importantly, his love for the Lord had never wavered.

"I always had the Bible open in our home," he said, as though trying to dispel his own doubts.

"Yes, dad, you did" I agreed, thanking him for the pearls of truth in Scripture he had revealed to me.

Sunshine lit up his voice after that, and I tried to end our conversation on a lighter tone.

"We'll be there Saturday as usual. Will you be able to make my yogurt for me?"

Dad, master yogurt-maker, assured me he would and as usual his last words were, "Be sure and bring the boys."

I laughingly promised him I would, replacing the receiver and sitting thoughtfully wondering why I had the distinct feeling that *he* was trying to keep a secret from *me*.

On Saturday morning we were awakened early by an

urgent call from mother asking us to come quickly; Dad had gone into shock. So soon, I thought, my heart heavy as we drove the freeways to their home. I was not ready. There was too much left undone, unsaid.

While our family gathered in the kitchen, I slipped quietly into my father's room and sat by his bed watching his face. He was not sleeping peacefully but rather had slipped into a half-coma, unaware of the whirling world around him.

As I took his large familiar hand and held it close, my mind went threading back to the times that hand had disciplined me, comforted me, and provided for me. As a child I had feared and resented him because of that strong hand of authoritative discipline, but maturity had brought a deepening love and understanding of the man he had been in our home.

I remembered that when I was a young mother unexpectedly pregnant with my fifth child he had been the one to assure me that children were God's gift, not to be rejected or taken lightly. He was glad, he had said, that I was going to have another baby and mischievously threatened that it had better be another boy. "I wish I had twelve sons, just like Jacob," he had smiled, his eyes twinkling.

My fifth child was a boy, the light of my father's life, the shadow in his footsteps.

"Dad," I said now, even though I didn't think he could hear me, "it's me, Margaret."

He awakened suddenly, turned as though he had known all along I was there, and looked directly at me like someone coming out of a deep sleep. "Well, hello, honey." His eyes were glazed, but his next statement assured me that his senses were intact. "Did I make enough yogurt for you?"

Yogurt! As sick as he must have been the day before he had kept his promise to make the usual batch of yogurt "because it's so good for you and the children."

"Yes," I said quickly. "Thank you, dad."

"It's all right," he said. "You're the best daughter I've got." It was a private joke between us, and for a moment before he slipped back into a coma, a smile lit up his face.

"And the only one." I began to cry softly over my answer to the parrying that had gone on between us for years.

But now he was gone again into the world of the dying. Saturday morning sounds were lost to his ears.

We stood numbly by while ambulance attendants placed him on a stretcher and carried him to the waiting vehicle. My thoughts were unsteady on the ride to the hospital. Dad would never see his beloved home by the ocean again. "A little heaven to go to heaven from" he would say gazing out at the blue expanse of the Pacific down through tiled roofs and tall palm trees.

Words sliced in and out of my thoughts. "What is your life? You are a mist that appears for a little while and then vanishes" (James 4:14 NIV).

At the hospital blood was pumped into his veins, and he began to rally.

"I'll stay with dad," Vern offered, and he did, sitting by my father's bedside throughout the long, uncertain night. And when dawn filtered through the hospital window, dad moved restlessly, calling, "Is that you, Vern?"

"Good morning, dad."

"I knew you were here, but I couldn't seem to say your name. Thank you for staying. I'll never forget it."

It was the first of many weeks of long nights.

"I want to go home." This was the third day, and dad

was feeling strong after a blood transfusion. "I don't need to be here." He was angry that his body was imprisoning him away from his beloved home.

But anger subsided when weakness invaded his body and white blood cells overpowered red ones, his head pounding like the surf against the sandy shores rendering him defenseless against the pain.

"I want to go home," he was still saying, only more faintly now, and if he could have finished the sentence it might have been "to die."

"My boys are coming to take me home," he insisted to the doctor.

"Not yet—not yet," the kindly man shook his head.

Dad's big frame settled back onto the bed in helpless resignation.

Sometimes during a fitful, coma-like sleep he dreamed he saw his long-dead brothers and talked with them in mumbled tones. One day he remembered his only living brother and began to weep. "I want to see my brother."

Nothing could dissuade him, not even a long-distance call. He needed his flesh-and-blood brother in the room with him; he was longing for the roots of his past in his final days. So his brother, a busy pastor from a large church in New York, came and sat by dad's bedside and read the comforting words of Jesus from John 14.

"Joe," he said, "the Lord has prepared a place for you."

One night when the pain was obviously weakening him greatly, dad said, "I talked to the Lord last night and told Him I want to go home. I have some things to do yet." Thus, his bargaining began and lingered for days.

He had to go home, he insisted, to care for his grapefruit tree, to plant new seeds in the vegetable garden.

I leaned close. "You've done so much already, dad. And the best thing you ever did was tell me about Jesus."

An inner candle lit up his suffering face, and within moments he fell peacefully asleep.

His worn Bible lay on the bedstand, and daily I opened it to read notes he had written in margins, or underlined verses of hope and comfort from painful years when he had traveled through personal grief and heartache.

One day he asked me to read a passage from the Bible, but his failing memory could not recall where it was.

"Lamentations" he finally said faintly.

So I began at the first chapter and read through.

"No," he shook his head.

The second chapter?

"No," he said.

I closed the Bible for he had fallen asleep.

Weeks after his death I found the verse dad had wanted to hear as he lay dying. My eyes filled with tears. Why hadn't I known? He had quoted it almost daily for as long as I could remember.

It was in the third chapter. I just hadn't read far enough.

> The Lord's lovingkindnesses indeed never cease,
> For His compassions never fail.
> They are new every morning;
> Great is Thy faithfulness (Lam. 3:22, 23 NASB).

On an early Sunday morning while the stars were still twinkling in the pink dawn, we were urgently summoned to the hospital.

Dad was in a coma, struggling to breathe, his throat choking with mucus. Machines were wheeled in, blood transfusions flowed, bottles were taped everywhere, and an oxygen mask was placed on his ashen face. In a few hours the crisis was over, and we went home to snatch a bit of sleep.

In the afternoon when I arrived at the hospital, dad was sitting up in bed, smiling as though he had a secret.

"You look marvelous," I said, sensing immediately that his restlessness was gone.

"I talked to the Lord last night."

"Last night?" I remembered his staring eyes, his labored breathing. "Last night?"

"Oh, yes," he assured me. "I knew you were standing right there and that my family was around. And while I was talking to the Lord, I told Him that now it is all right; He can take me Home."

His bargaining was over, and the sweet peace of acceptance had brought soul rest.

He waited until my mother came to tell his wonderful secret. "Last night I saw the angels from heaven coming for me. They were flying straight for this room when suddenly they turned back."

And we, who had been standing so close, had not heard a single rustle of angel wings nor a solitary note of that wondrous music from the heavenly choir.

Dad's glory trip was postponed four more days. But now the pain was lessened, and a song or a verse of Scripture would burst from his lips in praise. He had caught a glimpse of eternity and the glory shone in his face.

It was almost Father's Day, and we told him we were bringing a new robe as a gift. "No, honey," he said, pointing heavenward. "There's a robe waiting for me in glory. I'm going Home."

My last night with dad is a cherished memory. Vern

38

and I stood beside his bedside, a quiet kind of love lingering there between us.

A young nurse hurried into the room to take his temperature.

"This is my daughter." He nodded toward me. "The best one I ever had."

I kept the tears back somehow when I answered for the final time, "And the only one."

Dad wanted to sing, so the three of us held hands, and while Vern and I stumbled through some of the verses of his favorite hymns, dad's voice sang each word loud and clear: *"When I'm growing old and feeble, stand by me"* and *"Only glory by and by."*

We stayed until mother came to take our place, and as he took her face in his trembling hands he said huskily, "Well, mama, we've been together over fifty years."

He was saying good-by.

Vern and I turned to go, but I stopped briefly at the door. I was certain that this would be my last look at my father in this life.

"Good-night, dad," I said.

"Good-night, honey."

That night the angels completed their journey and carried my father safely Home.

Everyone is not given the sorrow and joy of watching a godly parent die, and I am deeply appreciative of those weeks for it was like finishing a painting or fitting the last pieces of a puzzle together.

I remember an incident one day on the hospital floor when I was visiting my father. I heard a woman's shrill cry, "Does anybody here know how to pray?" That same plea went on until I could stand it no longer. I walked to her bedside and leaned over, "I know how to pray. May I pray for you?"

But she couldn't answer. She was in a frenzied partial coma. I asked the Lord to bring peace to her soul and left, marking well the contrast between a person who had daily lifted his voice to heaven and one who did not know how to pray when prayer was what she needed most.

My father's doctor wrote my mother a letter after the funeral:

> I have been a physician for over thirty years. I have known many wealthy and famous people, but your husband is the first one who ever told me about God's love for me through Christ Jesus. He is the one who helped me in my groping faith to find Him.

Joy in
the Morning

# 3 Joy in the Morning

On the drive home after my father's funeral, I sat between my two teen-age daughters. I remember that Kathi's hand pressed warmly against mine. Never—never in my wildest imaginings could I have foreseen that the following year we would be weeping beside Kathi's graveside. At that moment I would have considered that grief beyond my endurance.

I remember clearly the blizzardy March morning of Kathi's birth. It had been a long, pain-filled night, and when the faintest light of dawn crept into the frosty sky, our second daughter was born, three weeks ahead of schedule. Perhaps this was a portent of things to come for

43

she was always in a hurry, not wasting a precious minute of time. We named her Kathleen Anne, and when her tiny hand grasped my outstretched finger, my delighted heart was captured.

As I recalled from the birth of our first daughter, Cindy, half the fun in the hospital was the bantering between young women sharing birthing experiences, exclaiming delightfully over newborn babies. Not so this time! My roommate turned away when I smiled and said hello, and all further attempts at conversation were similarly thwarted. She gazed grimly through the window at the steadily falling snow, her stormy mood matching the blizzard outside. In my contented happiness I didn't notice that her arms were empty while mine held my baby girl.

When I nursed Kathi, my roommate looked the other way. Later that afternoon her doctor strode into the room, stood stiffly by her bed, and said bluntly, "You won't be able to have your baby now. We're doing tests and should have the results by Monday."

"What—what is it—what do you suspect?" she asked, her face expressionless.

"We're not sure, but his muscle tone is very poor. It may be cerebral palsy or—" and he uttered a long medical term that sent chills up my back. My roommate's stricken face reflected grief's fresh and open wound.

"I don't believe him," she said when the doctor left. "There's nothing wrong with my baby. I just don't believe him." She repeated the words of assurance, but not to me; they were directed to the frosty window by her bed.

The next morning my husband came, dismissal papers in hand. We stood happily by while the nurse dressed Kathi in a newly crocheted sweater and bonnet, tying matching booties on her squirming feet. A white-fringed shawl was wrapped around her body twice, and while I sat gingerly in the wheelchair Kathi was gently laid in my waiting arms.

I turned to my silent roommate. "I'm sorry," I said softly. She half smiled and whispered, "Good luck with your baby."

Twenty-seven years have passed since that wintry day, and I have often wondered, Did that mother take her son home? Did he grow to be a man in a wheelchair? Was he severely handicapped? Or did he die as an infant? I will never know.

But I do know that parents of handicapped children so often bless our world, sharing the ways God's super-abundant grace has given then added strength. At first they cry, of course, but these same weeping parents later joyfully proclaim that their child was an angel unaware, a blessing they would not do without.

I remember Reggie Heibert, a young mother from central California. She approached me after a banquet where I had shared the story of our daughter Kathi.

## Reggie

"I have an only child, a boy just a little over a year old, who is dying of a brain tumor," she said, showing me her son Micky's picture. I asked Reggie to keep in touch, and she did. Her son lived until he was nearly four, longer than the doctors had anticipated. During the last months he suffered severe seizures, bleeding stomach ulcers, and problems that made it necessary for Reggie to suction his throat and nostrils and insert a feeding tube.

After Micky's death, Reggie wrote:

45

*I wondered why God allowed him to linger on in such a
hopeless condition, but then at other times I was so
thankful to have him, even in his awful state (which was
selfish on my part), and I wanted to keep him forever. I
knew God was planning everything and in His perfect
timing would take Micky at the best time. Just about
Easter I was ready to release Micky and prayed that God
would either heal him completely here on earth or heal
him in His divine way. But when Micky died I hurt more
than ever, knowing that no one can really prepare
for the death of a loved one. . . . I rejoice at the idea of
joining my baby someday, but I sure miss him now.
Growth takes a lot of patience, and growth must endure
hurt.*

Reggie also enclosed a letter she had written to Micky
ten days after his death. I want to share it with suffering,
empty mother arms everywhere:

*My dear Micky,*

*It has been well over a week since angels carried you to
the arms of Jesus, and my heart still aches like it did the
minute I received news of your death. Mom has been
doing a lot of thinking lately, as you can imagine. Even
though we were preparing for your journey to heaven, it
still seems hard to believe at times. I think of how strong
you were on earth and how much pain and frustration
you endured. You never complained. You are a special
son and always will be. When I was pregnant, somehow I
sensed you would be special. You know, like President of
the United States someday. Little did I know what a
wonderful plan God had for dad and me and especially
you. And the best part is that His plan continues.*

*Micky, you taught mom a lot, especially during the past
year. My love for you is so great that it overflows onto
each and every child I meet. I have become more*

46

sensitive to people's needs, especially people who are handicapped. You taught me to live in the present and not to ponder the past or swallow up my thoughts with the future. Most of all, you taught me about eternal life and heaven. What is a Christian who does not understand eternal life? She is a Christian incomplete. Now a part of me lives in heaven and my heart is at peace with the Lord, and my heart rejoices.

I read somewhere that life was not meant for the satisfying of a life for earth but for the development of a life for heaven. My, Micky, it only took you three and a half years, one month, and one day, to be exact! Although the span of your precious life was brief, you completed a mission, served a purpose, and performed a God-appointed task in this world. Now you have a perfect body and a wisdom mom cannot understand. To repeat the words of another parent, slightly changed, I say this to you, my darling son . . . "Your presence turned my thoughts to the best, your helplessness brought out my strength and protection and your loveliness and sweetness roused my tenderness and love.

No more worries for mom, no more prayers for you, Micky, for now you are where you belong, at home with the Lord, the greatest caretaker of all. I know you are still with me in a special way and you are telling me not to be sad, to only be happy because you are happy. Relatively speaking, it will not be long until I will be in heaven eternally with you, Micky, when I will hold you in my arms again. What a wonderful thought!

In closing, sweet man, I would like to share with you something someone else said of you: "If there was anything Micky knew, it was that he was loved by his mom and dad, all his family, and the two church families that touched him. It was beautiful to watch that love flow to him."

*I know you will have a special place in everyone's heart you touched and will continue to touch. I love you, Micky, now and forevermore.*

*Your Mom*

Micky's life was brief, filled with suffering, yet Jesus said, "Blessed (happy) are those who mourn, for they will be comforted" (Matt. 5:4). Reggie says she has mourned and will mourn, but there is a sweet comfort in the promise of a reunion in the eternal Home God has prepared for all those who love Him where she knows she will be with Micky again.

Often the handicapped child lives far longer than medical science would predict then the constant daily care that falls to the parent can create a tight bond of protecting love and a deeply rooted growth revealing God's sustaining grace in ways parents of healthy children may never experience.

Twenty-one years ago David De Boer was born, a victim of cerebral palsy. He is the fifth child of our friends Jay and Lois De Boer. When I was on a speaking tour in and around my hometown in Michigan one summer, the De Boers invited me to their home for dinner. I mentioned that I was writing this book about heartache and asked if they would like to share their thoughts on the subject.

### David

"Heartache?" Lois smiled. "Yes, I suppose at the beginning we would have called David's handicap that, but not any more. We've been greatly blessed and have already seen our 'weeping in the night' become 'joy in the morning.'

"But I remember those first months" she continued, "Long sleepless nights, a screaming baby, thinking he was simply fussy because he was premature. But slowly the thought took root that something was wrong—terribly wrong—with our baby. He would scream, arching his head to his heels in terrifying convulsions. Night after night I tried to keep him quiet so the family would sleep, feeding and rocking him until I was physically exhausted."

Jay nodded, remembering. "I knew Lois had come to the end of her strength the night she walked into our bedroom, placed David on the bed, and said, 'That's it. I can't handle it any more,' and walked away. Right then I decided we had to change doctors and find some answers. The new doctor placed David in the hospital and after extensive tests came up with the grave diagnosis of brain damage."

"How frightening that must have been," I said, but Lois shook her head slowly.

"It wasn't a total shock. There was a bit of premonition, because during my pregnancy I hemorrhaged so badly the doctor advised a theraputic abortion. We wouldn't do that, so we prayed, 'Lord, if it is Your will for this baby to be born, we accept that. And if not, You can take him any time.' That was our commitment, and it still is."

"We were given the usual advice," Jay said. "'Place him in an institution for the good of the family.' And for a time we wondered if we should. We made the preliminary preparations, signed papers, and—"

"We couldn't do it," Lois interjected. "We just couldn't. When we learned that David would only receive crib care there, we knew he would vegetate, so we picked him up and walked away. I told Jay on the way home 'I'll die taking care of David rather than leave him there.' "

Jay said, "On the drive home I kept thinking, God must have placed David in our home for a good reason."

"Have you ever wondered if the Lord might heal David?" I asked hesitantly.

"As both a pastor and a father of a handicapped son I have had to deal with that many times," Jay said. "My conclusion from Scripture is that God's ways are higher than our ways and that He has purposes for our lives that will help others and bring glory to Him. For instance, Lois and I have had opportunities to minister more effectively to others with handicapped children because of David.

"One day in the ward while we were waiting for the results of some tests I noticed a family standing together weeping their hearts out. I tried to comfort them, but the woman blurted out, 'Yes, it's easy for you to say, but that isn't your baby blind and helpless in that crib.' When I told her that my own son was lying in the bed next to her child's, she stopped weeping and the family began to respond immediately. They later made a decision to give their lives to Christ and great things happened in that home."

"After awhile," Lois said, "I began to ask, 'Lord, what is Your purpose for David going into the hospital this time? Who can I help?' I found that I was not only thinking about David but of others who were suffering, and that put things in a different perspective."

"When people ask how we can accept this, why we have peace," Jay added, "we tell them it's the inner working of the Holy Spirit and the perfect peace He gives when everything is committed to Him—even suffering."

I wondered if their other children had shown resentment toward David, and Jay answered.

"At one time our daughter did because she had to care for him often, so Lois and I agreed to talk with the children and let the whole family decide whether David should be placed in a home. We made it clear that if it were any one of them with a physical problem we would be facing the same decision. It wasn't long before everyone was weeping and the decision was made without a word. From that night on, David was fully accepted and there seemed to be no more resentment."

"Most people have been so accepting of him," Lois said. "Only one time stands out in my mind that David was badly hurt. When he was five, the girls took him to school in his first little wheelchair. We had it all worked out with the teacher, and David was so excited. But when he came home, he was quiet for a long time and finally blurted, 'Mommy, they think I'm crazy.' "

"People shy away from wheelchairs," Jay remarked, "as though the person couldn't be mentally competent because his body isn't totally functioning. But we are thankful for the people who have given real input into David's life, like his Sunday school teacher who led him to Christ. David understood clearly and wouldn't rest until he was baptized and gave his testimony before the church. He prays beautifully, often remembering things we forget. He prays faithfully for missionaries and ends his prayers with thanksgiving that he can do as many things as he can, remembering others who are totally helpless."

And then Jay talked of his concern for David's future and the home he and Lois plan to build for handicapped adults.

"We're going to call it 'David's House.' David means 'beloved' you know."

I did know for I have a David of my own.

"Many good things have come out of David's life," Jay continued. "Young people deciding to teach handicapped children, building this home where we can house many others like David, and our own personal growth through the years."

Lois ran her hand through her short, curly hair. "I remember the hours I grieved sitting and rocking David as a baby, weeping when I'd see a baby his age making normal progress, knowing David wouldn't ever go out on a date or play football or drive a car. We certainly do not know the reasons *why*—but that too is part of the life of faith, trusting even when we can't understand at all."

As I lay waiting for sleep that night, I thought of my own son David. Both David's were twenty-one years old, but how different their lives had been. My David was a powerfully built young man who raced into the house, the refrigerator his first goal, grabbing what was nearest at hand only to rush back to his car leaving behind a cloud of dust. David De Boer was a fair-haired gentle young man confined to a wheelchair.

Yet in many ways these young men were alike for they both loved God, wanted to serve Him and were equally loved by their heavenly Father.

I thought of some lines our David had written just before he turned twenty-one, a time when he was searching for God's plan for his life and reaching deep inside himself to be God's man. I was sure it was the prayer of David De Boer too: a desire that God would use his life in spite of his handicap, in spite of the wheelchair; a desire to be the very best man of God he could be.

> *My mind's cry is a restless sound,*
> *One that's piercing, deep in ground.*
> *It tells where my desires be,*
> *The sounding cry rings endlessly.*

> *I'm torn between my mind and heart,*
> *Conflicts that seem to tear apart.*
> *My mind longs for the new and bold.*
> *My heart returns to what is old.*
>
> *Lord, I need You to make of me*
> *A mighty instrument to be.*
> *Take my potential, use it, Lord.*
> *Make me like a mighty sword.*
>
> *I long for pleasant, perfect peace,*
> *Contentions in my life to cease.*
> *Make me like Christ, a useful man.*
> *I will be yours, the best I can.*

I thought of the eternal morning when all the Davids of this world will run free, their bodies no longer a prison, and God's promise came to my sleepy mind like the quiet of a flowing stream: "Weeping may endure for a night, but joy cometh in the morning" (Ps. 30:5 KJV).

You
May Give Them
Your Love, But
Not Your Thoughts

# 4 You May Give Them Your Love, But Not Your Thoughts

I was telling my friend Liz about David De Boer the following day. She had invited me to her lovely home for lunch, and because we hadn't seen each other since Vern and I had moved from Michigan twenty-one years before, we had a lot of catching up to do on the happenings in our lives.

"I wonder," Liz said, "if the suffering caused by a rebellious child isn't as deep, though in a different way." She was gazing at the pictures of her sons as she spoke.

"Gary and Brian are away at college," Liz said, "but Mike, the curly-haired one in the middle, was our rebellious son." Then Liz told me Mike's story.

*Mike*

Mike came of age during the Vietnam conflict, and he began to rebel against everything—our culture, our church, our authority as parents. Even though he had made a commitment to Christ and had been active in the youth group, he was studying godless philosophers, quoting idealistic teachers, turning away from the greatest Teacher of all. Mike could argue like a lawyer, and very subtly he began absorbing the philosophy of his generation—"If it feels right, do it."

Steve and I pointed out to Mike that this was dangerous, that what might seem right to one person could be against the law or very harmful to the lives he touched. We asked him where he would draw the line on doing his own thing and what basis he would use for measuring what was right.

One night we got into a terrible argument with him, all of us saying harsh things out of anger, pushing him further away. When he stormed out of the house, his clothes thrown over his arm, we thought he just needed a cooling-off time. But it was over five years before we heard from or saw him again.

What difficult, heartbreaking years! But during that time we learned how to pray, convinced that God would be about His business of revealing Himself to Mike wherever He was. I died a thousand deaths during those years, wondering where Mike was, if he was alive or dead. Every time the phone rang wondering if . . . and then the weeping in the night for the sound of his voice. Sometimes I'd be in a department store and tears would suddenly flow as I began wondering about my son, wanting so much to touch him, to tell him how we loved him.

Steve and I went through a self-condemning period—blaming ourselves, then each other—until finally we realized that unless we released Mike to God we would destroy our home. That was a turning point—learning to trust God when there was nothing to lean on, nothing we knew to do.

We realized that we had been too judgmental with Mike, so with Gary and Brian we avoided the trap of arguing as they entered their years of questioning.

Five difficult years went by. Then one day the phone rang. It was Mike!

"Mom" he said, and his voice was so dear my hands began to shake, "how would you like your wandering son back home?"

He was trying to make light conversation, but tears broke through his voice. I just broke down and said, "Oh, Mike, come home. We'll wire you the money to fly."

But he said he'd make it his own way, and the phone went dead. That boy hitchhiked all the way from the west coast to Michigan, arriving here in the middle of a blizzard when snow was piled so high we could hardly open the front door. But there he stood, cold and wet, his hair to his shoulders, a straggly beard, but, oh, those clear blue eyes looking questioningly at me. I hugged him, drawing him into the warmth of the house.

He showered, shaved, and ate like a man coming out of the desert. Gary and Brian were home because it was during the holidays, and they were so excited they didn't quite know how to show their exuberant thankfulness that Mike was back, so they challenged him to a game of Ping-Pong in our recreation room.

When Steve came home from work, he saw his three sons slamming that ball over the net as though they were in world competition. Steve began to weep for the first time since Mike had left.

When Mike and his father faced each other, I wondered what would happen. At first it was awkward with Mike extending his hand, but Steve reached over and grabbed him and they hugged for a long time. I guess you might say it was a weepy time for all of us.

After dinner we lit the fireplace and sat before its glowing warmth. While we drank hot apple cider, Mike told his story. At first I thought I didn't want to hear, really didn't wish to know, but it was healing for Mike to go back over those years—and healing for us.

He had been into drugs and living in a commune he told us, thinking it was heaven to be with others who shared his philosophy. But when he began missing some of his money and found he was being lied to and spied on, he became disenchanted. The leader of the commune was like a dictator demanding absolute loyalty, forcing the young people to turn over their money under threat of their lives. Sex was as casual as eating popcorn at a movie. Mike said he felt trapped and miserable so he ran away from there and changed his name.

He still was searching for the ideal life style where everyone could live on a higher consciousness of love, doing what they felt was right without infringing on another person's rights. Only it didn't work because often what was right to one person deeply harmed another.

The day Mike called home, someone he trusted had just robbed him of nearly all his belongings. He didn't know what our reaction to him would be, but when I cried "Mike, come home" he headed for the highway and hitchhiked his way home.

He told us that he had learned from experience that God lays down rules for our protection and good. Now Mike's faith is his own, not ours, not something he was taught to believe but a true commitment to follow Christ.

Liz was smiling when she finished her story. I glanced once more at the smiling boy in the photo. Like the prodigal son he had returned, and like the waiting father his parents had received him back. *And they didn't ask one question.* They had simply accepted him with unconditional love.

Unfortunately not all of life's stories end happily. There are many wandering children, teen-agers and adults, who have not made the journey back. Like Sara Hamilton.

## Sara

Sara and I were childhood friends. We were raised with the same strict upbringing, and during our early teens we both questioned and rebelled. I found no fulfillment in the pursuit of happiness in the world, and in my eighteenth year decided to follow Jesus Christ. Sara never did stop rebelling.

I lost track of her for a long time, my life busy with marriage and five children, but while I was back in my hometown recently, I visited her parents. I asked about Sara. Her mother dialed long distance to Sara's home and handed the telephone to me. I mentioned to Sara that I was calling from her parent's home, and after a distinct silence she resumed talking. We reminisced and laughingly remembered back to our childhood days of riding bikes, building bonfires on autumn days, ice-skating on the rink near our home where we'd nearly freeze before we'd race for home to get warm.

When I replaced the receiver, I turned to Sara's mother. "I'm sorry, she didn't ask—"

"It's all right," Mrs. Hamilton said sadly. "I didn't expect her to ask to speak to us. She hasn't communicated beyond an occasional 'hi' or 'good-by' in years."

Mr. and Mrs. Hamilton were never sure what they had done to cause Sara's hostility.

"She's had to eat the bitter fruit of her own rebellion," her mother said. "After she was married and had three children, she became involved with another man and left her home and family to live with him. Her husband took their children and left the state, and Sara hasn't seen them for years; she doesn't even know where they are. Her children are grown now and could locate Sara if they desired but have made no contact with her. She is heartbroken over losing contact with her children but doesn't realize that she herself is lost to us."

I remembered that saying, "Sooner or later whatever you have done to someone else will be done to you." Or in more profound words, "Whatsoever you sow, you will reap."

"We asked Sara's forgiveness for whatever it was we had done to cause her to turn away from us and the God we love," Mrs. Hamilton said.

"Perhaps," I suggested, "Sara has equated God with you and is really fleeing *Him*." Mrs. Hamilton nodded sadly.

Not long after that visit, my elderly friend suffered a severe heart attack and was hospitalized. Surely, I thought, now Sara will run to her mother, hold her hand, and plead for forgiveness. One doesn't rebel against an aging, ailing mother, does one? Sara did! She made only two hasty visits to her dying Mother. Mrs. Hamilton died without the touch of her daughter's hand on her arm.

"A foolish child is a grief to their parents," the wise Solomon said (Prov. 17:25).

But it is a grief which can be shared with a loving Lord who has many rebellious children of His own.

# Don't Give
# the Final Score
# at Half-Time

# 5 Don't Give the Final Score at Half-Time

In her book *Where Does a Mother Go to Resign*, my friend
Barbara Johnson tells of the heartache she has known on
her suffering road.

Years ago, Barbara's husband, Bill, was in an auto
accident and suffered brain damage. At that time she and
Bill had four young children. After years of prayer and
therapy—and contrary to medical opinion—Bill
recovered, but not before Barb had another taste of the
cup of suffering.

In 1968 one of their four sons was killed in Vietnam.
Five years later Barb was at the same morgue choosing a
casket for her firstborn son who had been killed in an

automobile accident on his way home from a trip to Alaska.

Barb writes of her joy even through grief and how the Lord used the deaths of her sons to bring many others to know Him.

But that was not Barb's greatest heartache.

The bottom rung of her sorrow came the day she found homosexual magazines in her son's room and confronted him with her knowledge.

"Yes, yes, I'm gay," her son, Larry, shouted as he ran out the door and out of his family's life for eleven months.

At that time, Barb couldn't find a single mother who would admit her child was homosexual, so she vowed she would become that mother.

Barb told me what happened.

## Barbara

I felt amputated, as though someone had cut off part of me. I was so *alone* in the situation, as though there were no other mothers in the world with a gay son. But instead of being alone, I found I was only part of a heartbroken minority scattered everywhere in the world. It would have been far less of a jolt if I had known other parents who could have helped me through my initial suffering.

After counseling and prayer and a deep walk through the valley I realized that Larry wasn't a tragedy but the same son who had brought us joy and blessing through the years.

The love and compassion I had so easily displayed before had to be there for Larry to see. Bill and I wanted him to know we were loyal and that we still loved him as our son.

I was reminded of God's unconditional love to us; He doesn't withdraw His love when we fall into sin. And we should not withdraw our love from Larry. We hated the sin, because sin hurts God and hurts us, but by letting our love flow, we could prevent stagnation and bitterness from settling in our hearts and could insure Larry of this unconditional love which we hoped would remind him of God's love toward him.

I had often counseled people telling them that trials were to strengthen the bonds of their faith, making them strong as cables. Now God turned it around and reminded me that this trial was to deepen my faith. How often I had glibly quoted Romans 8:28: "All things work together for good to them that love God." Now I had to prove that it was true in my own life or I would be a hypocrite. Could even Larry's homosexuality work together for good?

Bill and I have had to stop blaming ourselves. We've learned that we cannot accept the blame or credit for the choices our children make. After studying the believed causes of homosexuality, we found them so diversified that no one factor could be called the root cause.

It can be devastating to read or hear that homosexuality is caused by a domineering mother–absent father, but that is one of Satan's tricks—to cut off the peace and love of the whole family because of the sin of one member.

We gave Larry to God, totally and irrevocably, and got down to the business of moving out of shock and into a productive situation for the rest of the family.

I collected verses, poems, helpful prose and put them in a shoebox called "My Joy Box." Then when heavy depression settled like a thick fog I read over what I had saved and gathered strength to carry me through dark days and nights.

Today Barb is ministering, counseling, and reaching out to parents of homosexuals. She has formed a group called "Spatula"—"for parents who are on the ceiling."

Barb and I parted with a promise to keep in touch. I received a letter from her the following week, and the truth of what she wrote has stayed with me through tough circumstances of my own.

> *The more broken-hearted I became, the more understanding I was of the cry of other bleeding hearts because I had tasted the cup of suffering.*
>
> *The Bible says that suffering is a necessary ingredient in our spiritual development. God says we are to glory—not only endure, but glory—in suffering and tribulation. The greatest comfort I have is that you cannot give the final score at half-time; the game is not over yet with God.*

**When
the Party's
Over**

## When the Party's Over

Tiny little bottle,
Tiny little pills,
Where's the peace you promised?
Where's the dream fulfilled?

Do you have the secret?
Can you pass the test?
Or are you cruel and haunting,
Heartless like the rest?

I know that I'm demanding,
But see how deep my pain.
Can you reach inside me
And take away the stain?

And what of all my memories?
Can you make me brave?
Or will I slowly, surely
Become your willing slave?

See how much I need you?
See what faith I hold?
I believe your promise.
My heart is sure and bold.

*But when the party's over*
And I need you once again,
Will you be my savior?
Will you be my friend?

# 6  When the Party's Over

If anyone had given the score at half-time in another Barbara's life, it would have been zero.

My first impression the day I met Barbara Copelan was that she resembled a model on her way to a fashion show rather than a young woman attending a small Bible study. Our mutual friend, Carol, had asked if I would teach a few girls at her home, and I had agreed.

Barbara was the first one to walk into Carol's house that day. She was elegantly tall and attractive with soft auburn hair, cut in the latest fashion, framing her exquisite features. Long silky lashes fringed large brown eyes that seemed closed against intrusion into her most private world.

It seemed inconceivable from the looks of her that day that Barbara would become one of God's most teachable servants, but as weeks passed and the balm of God's Word was poured into past wounds, healing her memories, she emerged from a long, dark journey into glorious light.

Though I learned bits and pieces of her story throughout the four years our group met, one day we sat together over tea and Barbara related her entire story to me.

## Barbara

My first memory is of Sale, Cheshire, England, a suburb of Manchester with lined-up government houses in rows of blocks; two-story homes were given to larger families like ours and one-story houses were rented to people with fewer children.

But only a ten-minute drive into the Cheshire countryside were rolling green hills, leafy elms, huge oaks and chestnut trees, and flowers wildly splashing brilliant colors everywhere. On each side of the road were fields of grass, freshly green from gentle, sometimes ceaseless, rains.

Our house was alive with children, eight in all, me being third in line. Because I was shy and withdrawn, some people considered me a snob. Actually I was usually quaking inside, fearful I might say something wrong and be shamefully embarrassed. How I wished I could be like my pretty outgoing sisters: turn my straight, mousy brown hair, bobbed in the most unbecoming fashion, into golden curls and think up clever things to say. Then maybe my parents would notice that their Barbara wasn't such a dull one after all.

I would have done anything to bring a smile to mum's tired face. But somehow I never measured up to whatever it was my parents expected, or I didn't think I did, which is really the same thing.

That little girl with the drab-colored hair and made-over clothes was crying out, "Look! Notice me! Listen, please listen!" But ears always seemed tuned to someone else. The child within still clamored for attention long after I was grown, and perhaps that's why my life took the course that it did.

Mum said to me once, "Barbara, you're so tall and skinny, the only thing you'll be good for is modeling." And because everyone told me I had become quite a pretty teen-ager, I quit school at fifteen and signed with a local modeling agency.

What a beautiful, fascinating world opened up to me: fashionable clothes, enchanting people, and parties where liquor flowed like water and everyone sparkled. I hadn't known such a life existed, and it was even more exciting that I, a poor girl from the country, could be a part of this world. The only drawback was my shyness and my inability to feel any self-worth or confidence.

For me the answer seemed a quick and magical one: sparkling champagne or wine flowing in abundance at the lavish parties the agencies arranged. I could be anybody then, a movie star, even a queen, holding a crystal goblet in my hand and laughing up at a tall, handsome stranger.

We models were told to be nice to the men at parties because they were influential, and if that meant drinking with them it was fine with me. As long as I had several drinks and a full glass in my hand I could speak out with confidence and be the life of the party; I could forget the little girl who never had more than

73

two dresses in her life and wore her sister's shoes.

At those parties I could be somebody and loved the feeling. I drank anything, the stronger the better, and when someone told me vodka couldn't be detected on your breath I began carrying a plastic bottle in my purse in case I needed a sudden surge of confidence on my way to a modeling job. It was so easy to slip into the ladies room, take a nip before boarding the subway, and lift my courage to face the day. It was a new, exhilarating way of life, modeling during the day, drinking and partying at night. I was accepted at last—or so I thought.

Nearly every model in Manchester dreams of moving on to the big-city glamour of London, and that was my goal too. When I finally signed with a London modeling agency, I thought I was at the top!

Modeling is hard, tedious work, fiercely competitive, and though I didn't know it, or wouldn't admit it, I began turning to liquor to blot out my fears and insecurities. In fact, liquor was becoming the most important thing in my life, my leaning post. Sometimes when I was waiting in the lobby of the agency for an assignment, the other girls would stare at me, and I'd smile inwardly, imagining they were envious of how nice I looked. Now I know they were staring because I was tipsy.

There's something about drinking that makes you crave water during the night, but instead of reaching for a glass of water I'd drink more booze, forcing it down my throat even though I was violently nauseous. I was beginning to have troubling thoughts as I lay there, unable to sleep: *maybe I couldn't stop drinking even if I wanted to.* To drown out these thoughts, I had to drink heavier in order to fall asleep.

I was twenty-one when I met Al Copelan. He was working at a missile base near London, and I thought he

74

was a handsome, rich American. How lucky I felt when he searched me out at a party and asked me to dinner. Al and I became a twosome then, partying, going to theaters, to the pub at night with other couples, crowding into small booths, laughing at each other's jokes, ordering more drinks from the bar. That was the whole point! Your glass could never be empty.

It was the nights that made my life intolerable, unable to sleep, tossing and turning from side to side, and an elusive something within, gnawing away keeping my thoughts alive with turmoil.

I certainly didn't think about God; and Jesus Christ was only a swear word as far as I knew. I didn't think about any kind of afterlife or religion at all. Life was NOW. There was nothing to live for except "happiness" for the moment, and for me that was drinking, partying, modeling, and Al.

When Al told me he had to return to the United States, my heart sank. We said good-by at the airport, promising to write, but I didn't think I'd ever see him again.

After he was gone, life lost its luster. Modeling jobs weren't coming my way as often because word had spread that I had a drinking problem and the agency gave the work to other girls.

It was at this low point in my life that a friend wrote from Canada asking if I would come and share an apartment with her. She promised to help sign me with a modeling agency. Because I'd had it with my life in London, I began making plans to leave. Anyway, Canada was one step closer to my big dream, the United States, so I scraped up enough fare, packed my clothes, said a hasty good-by to my family, and flew to Toronto.

It was my second big move, and for the second time I was plunged into despair. Oh, the agency signed

me up and at first gave me jobs, but soon they were
elusive and wouldn't answer my telephone calls because
complaints were coming in about the model who showed
up half-tipsy. Why had I thought moving to another place
would change anything or help me stop drinking or make
any difference in the way I felt about myself?

One late wintry afternoon I was in a fancy restaurant in
Toronto having a few drinks by myself when a
good-looking man sat down at my table and began talking
to me. This happened quite often so I wasn't surprised
until he said casually, "Do you like beautiful clothes?"

I smiled my answer.

"You can have a wardrobe of clothes, all the clothes you
want."

"What do I have to do?" I asked.

"Just sit in a bar where I'll send you, and when a man
comes in and talks to you, go with him and do what he
wants. Then all those clothes will be yours."

I knew what he meant all right, but I kept thinking
about those beautiful clothes so I said I would do it.

"Do you have any money now?" he asked, reaching for
his wallet.

For some reason I said "yes," although in reality I was
broke. I didn't want him to know just how penniless I was
so I let him think I was a busy model with a good income.
He bought me a few drinks and left, after setting a date for
me to go to a certain bar.

The day came, and I sat in my room drinking heavily,
trying to gather courage to go. Jobs weren't coming to me,
the rent was due, and my only food was what my
roommate provided.

Several times I tried to leave for the bar, but it was like
another hand was holding me back. Now I know whose
Hand it was!

I lay on my bed crying and drinking until I fell asleep.

I couldn't hold a modeling job any longer because of complaints about my drinking, and when I was thrown out of my rooming house because I couldn't pay the rent, humiliation stung deeply, further damaging my already poor self-image, sending me running for the bottle.

Also, I had fallen in love with a man in Toronto, thinking I was loved back. I was warmly happy when he took me to meet his parents. But they took one look at me and disapproval waved before my eyes like a red flag. They noticed my glassy stare and wavering walk and dismissed me as not worthy of their very proper son.

I drank through that night trying to blot out the image of his parents' haughty, self-righteous manner.

But still we made plans for a life together. I trusted him; he would be the somebody I had always wanted to lean on.

Wrong again! When I was really in trouble, down so low, ill, out of work and needing help desperately, he walked out. I vowed I would never trust anyone again.

Rejection was no longer a quiet thing but a rushing, maddening torrent like a mountain waterfall. When I was well again, I paced my room for several days, yearning for the ring of the telephone, for his voice telling me," It's all right. I love you," but the days passed and the silent instrument mocked me. Sobbing and drinking, threads of thoughts were taking form. By the end of the week I had planned my own death.

When my roommate went out for a long evening, I decided to slash my wrists and end my miserable life. That called for a drink, then two, then three until I lost count. The razor's sharp blade blurred, but even so I shut my eyes tight against the spurt of bright red blood.

I stumbled onto the bed, hiding under several blankets, hoping when my roommate returned she would think I was sleeping. When morning came, I would be dead.

Again another Hand was on mine, because as I was lying under those blankets my hand slipped out, and when my roommate came home unexpectedly early she saw blood dripping onto the floor and quickly called the ambulance.

I heard sirens in the far corners of my mind. Then there were urgent voices in a hospital emergency room, and doctors and nurses were standing around my bed asking questions, but I couldn't move my lips to answer. When I was left alone, a flood of disappointing tears splashed down my face. I couldn't do anything right, not even die.

No one came to visit except my roommate. I was certain that the other people at the boarding house were thinking, "Oh, that alcoholic, she doesn't count for anything anyway." I didn't want to go back to that room and face the other tenants who knew I had tried to end my life. Weak from loss of blood and mentally coiled into a tightly wound ball, I begged the doctor to allow me to stay in the hospital a bit longer. He shook his head firmly, "No, Barbara, you're well now. You have to go out and face the world."

I walked back into that rooming house holding my head high, ignoring the stares of the other boarders. And there on my dresser was a letter from Al, who had been writing to me all this time, and who thought I was a popular, successful model. My spirits lifted. He said he was coming to Canada to see me the following week.

I rested, stopped drinking, got a proper haircut, bought a new outfit, and resolved to look successful and happy. I decided to ask Al if he could help me get a start in the United States where I could continue my search for that

78

perfect life; surely if there was such a utopian life it would be in America.

I didn't have to ask Al anything because he had been in Canada for only a day when he proposed marriage. I remember thinking "Why not? He's kind and treats me with respect—better than my other boyfriends." It sounded like my idea of heaven—to be securely married, to live in America where dreams came true just like in the movies.

I packed immediately, and we caught the next plane out of Toronto. Wouldn't it have been nice if I had been the proper kind of lady Al had described when he told his parents about me? Then I could have smiled at them securely, knowing I was worthy of their dear son. Instead, my nerves were raw and tender, still stinging from the rejection by the family in Canada.

Al's family was Jewish, close-knit and loving, and they reached out to accept me—the English model, popular and sought-after, so right for Al. I swallowed hard against my inadequacies, weaving a tighter web of pretense around me.

We had a small wedding and moved in with Al's parents for a month before buying our own place; this made the game of pretending even harder. Every day I said primly that I was going for a walk to exercise. And walk I did, traipsing up one unfamiliar block after another searching out a liquor store, buying a bottle of whiskey to drink on the way home to bolster my courage to play-act the role Al had unwittingly cast for me.

We bought our first little home, painted yellow with an English look to it with ivy climbing a white porch trellis and large blooming roses planted along the drive. It was the first time in my life I had had a place of my own, and while we were moving in and furnishing it I drank very little.

I went to work in an office to help buy some things for the house, and it wasn't long before I was involved in office parties, stopping off with the girls for a few drinks after work. It was easy to get the men in the office to buy us drinks to help unwind after a busy day. Suddenly I realized that here in perfect America people were just as desperate in their search for happiness and meaning to life as anywhere I had been.

Al and I began having communication problems in our marriage, sometimes not speaking to each other for two weeks at a time. I was easily hurt, the old rejection patterns surfacing. Lashing out at Al in anger and bursts of temper only intensified my need to stop off for drinks after work.

We both wanted a baby badly, so when I learned I was pregnant, I was ecstatic. Now I would settle into a new role and quit drinking so my baby wouldn't be harmed. All day I fought against walking to the cupboard and reaching for the bottle. I could restrain myself because my "reward" drink was waiting at the end of the day. I sipped it slowly just before Al came home for dinner.

Our beautiful daughter Stephanie was born, perfect and lovely, large brown eyes looking up at me in pure innocence. "I'm going to be a good mother, luv," I whispered. "I'll stop drinking, and you and I will be ever so close."

For a while it was true. But the slightest look of rejection from Al and back to the bottle I went, soothing my trampled feelings with the warm liquid flowing into my veins, blotting out the memory of the little girl I had been, looking in from the outside, never quite belonging.

I hid my bottles in shoes and boots, so Al never knew

80

how heavily I was drinking during the day.

Again the bottle became my best friend.

When Stephanie was nearly a year old someone told me about a job I could get as a cosmetics consultant. It sounded great—time away from the house, extra money of my own, and a surging hope that maybe this time the aching hole in my life would be filled.

But to go to sales meetings, meet new people, and conduct classes I needed confidence, so my friend the bottle went along. And there were the pills. Tranquilizers to calm me during the day and liquor to put me to sleep at night. When I wasn't sedated I was drunk, and when I wasn't drunk I was depressed. I felt so low I would lay helplessly on the floor—there seemed no place lower—weeping with weakness and self-loathing.

After cosmetic classes I'd go to a bar with the girls. Dancing and drinking, I threw off my cares and anxieties in the only way I knew. But driving home during wee hours of the morning, loneliness rode with me.

A friend told me about a self-improvement course that might help overcome my feelings of inadequacy and shyness so I went through the whole seminar. When it was over, I was like a person saved from drowning only to discover I was dying of something else.

This same friend gave me books on reincarnation, explaining that it was all right if I wasn't perfect because someday after my death I could come back and be somebody else.

It sounded so beautiful and right. She had statues of angels around her apartment, and just looking at them made me sad. One time I asked, "If I'm good enough, maybe around Christmas could I see God?"

"Yes, Barbara," she answered, "that's possible. It is possible to see God."

So that became my goal: being good enough to see God. I read all the books, but there was no peace in the thought that someday I'd be somebody else. I wanted to be somebody *now*.

Then I heard about a place near the ocean where you could sit and meditate. It was a long way from my home through winding canyons, but I drove there three times a week to sit on an isolated bench and meditate. I was told to chant the same word over and over until a light appeared in my forehead. That meant I had attained a high level of meditation. I strove for that goal with every bit of purpose I had, chanting with closed eyes, searching for the end of the rainbow—peace of mind.

I tried so hard to have meditation satisfy my deep longing for something better, but nothing filled the vacuum in my heart which was as deep and wide as the ocean.

And because meditation didn't work, I began drinking heavily once more.

Stephanie was four now, and during those days when I lay drunken on the sofa, crying in great sobs, she sat close, covering me with a blanket, putting a cold cloth on my head, her arms clasped tightly around my neck. "Why are you crying, mommy. I love you," she'd whisper. Stephanie quieted my weeping as I held her close, grateful for the one person in this world who loved me just as I was.

Al couldn't cope with my problems and his own difficulties on the job, so his solution was to pretend nothing was wrong. The only link between us was Stephanie whom we both adored. She was the only reason I didn't try to take my life again.

Selling cosmetics at the home classes did give a purpose

to life, because if you sold a certain amount you received
an award at the annual banquet held in a fancy hotel. It
was an exciting evening, the women dressed in their most
glamorous gowns. Even the atmosphere sparkled with
charm. When my name was called and I walked to the
podium to receive my award, just for that moment I was
the somebody I longed to be.

I noticed that some of the girls in the company were
different in a way I couldn't understand. They grouped
together, laughing and talking, without drinks in their
hands; yet they bubbled as though they had champagne
flowing from the inside. Maybe they were rich or happily
married or had sold a lot of cosmetics that month I
decided.

Donna was one of these girls, and one day she asked me
to go to a prayer meeting at the manager's house.

"A prayer meeting?" I asked. "What is it? What do you
do?"

"Just come along. You'll see," she smiled assuringly.

I thought I would go because if it was at the manager's
home. Important people would be there, and it was
always good to be with them to improve your status with
the company.

I didn't know what to expect, maybe like a seance or
something, but it was a living room filled with women
talking about God and Jesus like they knew Him. They
had sweet welcoming smiles for me, even those who
didn't know me. And no one was drinking.

They prayed right out loud to God like He was in
the room, and they talked to Him about their marriages
and children. I sat apart watching, my eyes wide-open;
beneath my lashes tears were longing to flow,
but I held them back resolving not to weep in that room.
But on the drive home the burst of tears began and lasted

on and off for three days. Every time my mind went back to that room of women looking so fresh and secure, I'd start to cry again. I didn't feel worthy to even be in the same room with them, and my already-plunging self-image sank to a new low.

A week went by—seven days of weeping over my troubled life and my crumbling marriage.

The following Saturday I stopped by my friend Carol's to pick up my weekly cosmetic supply. Carol had also been at the prayer meeting, and when we sat down I blurted out, "Carol, tell me. I have to know. How can I find God?"

I knew if there was anyone in this world who could give me the answer it was strong, secure, happy Carol with the vibrant personality and dancing sea-green eyes whose life seemed perfect. Now she looked directly at me and said without hesitation, "Barbara, God can only be found through Jesus Christ."

I didn't know why the sound of His name made me weep again. "What do I do this time?" I sighed, thinking this was another religion or form of meditation.

Carol took my hand and said simply, "Barbara, just receive Jesus into your life."

"How?"

"Ask Him. He says if you will open your heart, He will come in and make you a new person. I'll say a prayer, and you can repeat it after me if that's what you want. It's not an easy road, Barbara, but it's the only one to God."

I nodded, and Carol slipped to her knees. I knelt awkwardly beside her. When Carol said a few simple words, I repeated them tearfully. She asked God to make a brand-new person which was the cry from my own heart because I had tried everything I knew to change and nothing had worked.

When we sat back on the sofa, I waited for something miraculous to happen like maybe a great light from heaven or a vision of God, but the quietness in the room swept through my body filling me with peace.

"Carol," I whispered, "is it true? Will I really be a brand-new person? Can I receive a life that will be different? Will I stop drinking?"

I'm so glad Carol had the wisdom to say what she did that day. She didn't make enormous promises or tell me life would be all sweetness and light from that minute on. Quite the contrary, she explained that even though my new life had begun from the minute I asked Jesus into my life, the next step was very important. I must stay close to the Lord, obeying His Word. I was to expect trials and not be surprised if my old friends dropped me or if Al became hostile toward me. The difference would be that now Christ would walk through the rough places with me.

She said that forevermore God would not look at my past sinful life but at *Christ in me* who was holy and perfect, making me righteous in God's sight.

I didn't understand most of what Carol said that day, but one thing I remember clearly: "Barbara," she said, "think of yourself as a newly planted seed. It must take root and be watered in order to grow."

She also read Jesus' words: "Come to me, all you who are weary and burdened, and I will give you rest. Take my yoke upon you and learn from me, for I am gentle and humble in heart, and you will find rest for your souls" (Matt. 11:28, 29).

*Soul rest!* Of course. That was what I had been looking for all my life. And then I knew my long search was over. Now I know it was the indwelling Holy Spirit assuring me

of forgiveness the moment I opened my life to the Lord
Jesus Christ.

I wanted to tell somebody straightaway, and Donna
was the first person I called. When she said she had been
praying for me and had a gift saved up for this day
and would be right over, I wondered what the gift could
be. When she brought in the gift-wrapped box, I opened
it eagerly.

It was a Bible. I stared at the pages after Donna left, not
knowing where to read and unable to understand
what it all meant. So I just carried it around the house.

I wish I could say everything came right immediately,
that I quit drinking, but nothing quite so miraculous
happened. When Al and I went to his office parties and
the liquor was served, my body tensed and my mouth
went dry from wanting a drink so badly.

One time a man asked if I refused wine because of my
religion. I stiffened, and not wanting him to think I was
strange, I said I would take half a glass. But, of course, it
became a full glass, then two and three until I couldn't
stop at all.

I came home from those parties crying, feeling I had let
Somebody down. But every time we went to another
party the merry-go-round started again. I vowed not to
drink and came home dead drunk and deeply depressed
because now I knew I could not quit on my own.

I kept a bottle hidden high on the kitchen shelf, and
when Al and I would fight or things went a bit wrong in
my life I could reach for it.

"God," I prayed, "don't let me drink this. I don't want
to solve my problems this way." But always I'd be back at
the cupboard reaching for the magic way out through
alcohol.

Carol invited me to a Wednesday morning Bible study,

and the girls were so friendly and at peace with God. When they invited me to lunch with them, I so wanted to go, but backing away I explained I had to rush home. Where I was really running to was to a bar for an afternoon drink.

One day while sitting in a booth drinking, something seemed to illumine the dreary place and I could clearly see loneliness in the faces of the people around me. My own insides were exposed too. I, who was supposed to have a new life, was no different from them. I walked unsteadily from that bar, and I never entered another one. I had taken my first faltering step. But I couldn't stop drinking at home.

Al said, "Well, now you have this big God to help, prove how strong you are by quiting your drinking."

Where *was* this new life I was supposed to have? Why did I crave the warmth of liquor flowing down my throat?

The teacher from the Bible study was the first person to counsel me, explaining that there *was* power from God and He had given the Helper, the Holy Spirit, to fill and control my life if I would surrender to Him.

I wept as I told her my story, reliving childhood memories of rejection and shyness, the beginning of my drinking, the days when modeling jobs were given to other girls, rejection from the man in Canada, my attempted suicide, marriage problems that seemed unsolvable.

She listened, quietly taking my hand when I was through, and began to pray, asking God to go back with me through my life and heal every hurt, bind up every wound, asking that I would know I was worthy because God had accepted me. She prayed for my marriage that it would be brand-new and that God would take away the craving for alcohol.

I never drank again after that day.

The seed was taking root, and God was sending His children to water it, but as yet not a tiny shoot of green could be seen.

Al had been through so much with me, living with my drinking and temper tantrums. I knew he and Stephanie had suffered. Now I was anxious for him to see my changed life.

I did what many new Christians do. I became overly zealous—talking about God all the time, leaving books and literature around the house, hoping Al would read them, going to church three times a week, chatting away about my Bible studies. Al didn't show a flicker of interest. In fact, I'm sure he was tuning me out when I talked about my new faith. To him it was just another phase I was going through.

His only words were, "You'll never see me going to your church, so forget it."

One of the girls at the Bible study said, "Barbara, picture Al walking to church with you, a Bible under his arm." The idea seemed incredible, but our group began praying for that very thing.

I had joined a large church where the Word of God was preached so clearly that even I could understand. One day I made an appointment with the pastor, and he graciously took time to counsel with me.

"Parson," I said, sitting primly in his office, "I want my husband to know Jesus like I do, but he's indifferent. He doesn't care."

He spoke words of wise advice. "Barbara," he said, "don't *tell* Al about Christ; *show* him. Don't try to win him by words, but by your life. If you will read 1 Peter 3 every day and obey what it says, it will make a difference. And remember, God loves Al too."

That was a new thought: that maybe God was seeking Al and guiding his life the way He had sought mine. I did what my pastor said: I read 1 Peter 3 every day, put away my literature, and soon Al was perking up, noticing a difference in my attitude toward him.

One night a year later, Al told me he was going out for the evening. He returned at one o'clock in the morning and sat on the edge of our bed until I was fully awake.

"Well, where have you been?" I asked.

Then he told me how he, too, had felt a deep need in his life. That night he had gone to Carol's home and after visiting a bit with Carol and her husband Ralph, he began asking questions, the same questions I had asked the year before. Ralph and Carol carefully explained who Jesus Christ was, how He had been prophesied in the Old Testament, and that He was the Messiah of Israel. They had made God's plan of salvation very clear, and Al had accepted Christ as his Savior. Now he was a believer too!

The words of 1 Peter 3 flooded my mind: "Your godly lives will speak to [your husbands] better than any words" (1 Peter 3:1, 2 LB).

Al and I stumbled along our path of faith, but at least we were going in the same direction, learning and studying God's Word. Stephanie was six when she asked Jesus into her life with childlike faith.

Now when Al walks beside me to church, a Bible under his arm, I remember how the girls at the Bible study prayed for that very thing.

I cringe when I hear someone say, "Come to Jesus and your problems will be over." Not true! Of course, the major barrier of sin separating us from God is forever settled, but Christians, especially new believers, are often a favorite target of the enemy, Satan. He knows our weak places and shoots his arrows where we are most vulnerable.

Al and I had a windfall of testings almost immediately, but with each trial we grew to understand that no matter how deep the water, how hot the fire, the Lord walked through the hard times with us.

I've written my family in England, sharing my joyous new life, and though they might say, "Our Barbara has gone daft with religion," I don't lose heart. I've seen the power of prayer and what my heavenly Father can do in drawing others to Himself.

Seven years have passed since I said that brief prayer with Carol, words I hardly understood. And now with praise and thanksgiving I can say, "Yes, it's true. I *am* a new person, and at last—at last I have found peace."

Barbara concluded with a radiant smile, but her story isn't over yet; it's just begun. Whenever I catch a glimpse of her hurrying through the crowded patio at church, a friend next to her (she has an uncanny gift for finding the lost and lonely and befriending them), I remember the confused, troubled Barbara who was and rejoice in the Barbara who is.

She shares her story honestly at Christian Women's Clubs, is active in the Evangelism Explosion program, and she, who didn't know how to find one passage to read in the Bible just a few short years ago, is discussion leader in Bible Study Fellowship.

Barbara is no longer filled with wine but with the Holy Spirit, speaking out with confidence and boldness. She can turn a friendly "good-morning" from a stranger into a conversation about her love for Jesus and what He has done in her life. If the person is heartsick or lonely (Barbara has a way of finding that out), she nods and says,

"Yes, yes, I understand. I've been there. I know how you feel—lonely and searching, with troubling thoughts in the middle of the night—but listen—listen and I'll tell you something wonderful that happened to me."

Barbara has truly found the answer, and it wasn't at the bottom of a bottle. Her search ended when she didn't *do* anything but believe and receive God's wonderful gift of life and love through Jesus Christ.

When I asked Barbara what the most precious passage in the Bible was to her, she didn't hesitate: "Psalm 139," she said, smiling softly. "To think that God knew me and loved me even before I was born, and all the time I was down and confused and didn't think one thought about Him—well, then I say with King David, 'Such knowledge is too wonderful for me.'"

"I was like the woman at the well. My thirst was not for earthly water, even though I thought it was. I was craving *heavenly living water* so that I would never, never thirst again."

**Journey into Darkness**

# 7 Journey into Darkness

When I told my friend Ginger I was writing a book about heartache, she asked quickly, "Would you like a chapter on mental illness?"

I was silent a moment as my mind went racing back to my childhood and the heartbreak of a girl named Leanna.

Leanna worked in our home as a part-time maid during the 1930's. Leanna's work days meant fun for me. Even when she was down on her knees dusting along the edge of the brightly flowered rug she was talking, telling fascinating stories, her brown eyes dancing with merriment.

I don't remember just when Leanna began laughing too

loudly and long, anxiously bursting into hysterical tears, but I do recall my parents making a hurried phone call to our pastor to ask him to visit Leanna's home. My parents went with him, and I went along.

When we saw her, there wasn't a glint of recognition in her eyes. Instead, she had rather a vacant stare, and her once-beautiful chestnut hair was straggly and disheveled, falling into her face.

A short time later, Leanna was taken away to a state hospital and kept in a padded cell. The once-beautiful, merry Leanna had become hopelessly insane.

Little was known about mental illness then. In fact, that phrase "mental illness," was not coined until years later. "Crazy" was the word I remember. And the mentally ill usually were not spoken of again. If they were, they were discussed in careful whispers.

And so when Ginger seemed so willing to share the heartache she had endured, I agreed it was a story that should be told.

She spoke directly, a lifetime of grief behind her, telling the story of a young love that had turned into sudden madness and nearly plunged an entire family into mental instability.

## Ginger

The night the unmistakable smell of smoke wafted into our bedroom where I lay tossing and turning, trying to sleep, terror turned my blood cold. I raced to the kitchen. Standing there, a match in his hand, watching the flames leap through the curtains, was my husband Ed.

Trembling, I filled the nearest pan with water and doused the blaze. Ed stood expressionless as though he were in another world, and with a final thud of acceptance

I acknowledged what I had for so long tried to deny: I was married to a very sick man. The past years of his instability and wavering moods had been a journey into madness. Our life had become a crazy nightmare, unbelievably haywire.

I sat down and looked hopelessly at Ed who shrugged and wandered off to bed, mumbling, "Why not set fire to the house? Insurance companies have more money than they can ever use."

Ed fell asleep immediately, still angry that I had spoiled his brilliant plan for making a quick dollar. I sat through the night watching until it was morning and time to awaken the children.

How could I, a woman nearing thirty with four children to care for, be so helplessly trapped? Where had it begun? The whole dizzying, sickening film of my life played before my eyes as surely as though I were watching a full-length movie on a large screen.

I grew up during World War II days when the world suddenly turned topsy-turvy; strangers met and married within weeks or even days; values changed; future plans were accelerated because of the raging war that was stealing away our carefree youth, forcing us into adulthood long before we were ready.

I met Ed when he was a seventeen-year-old sailor on leave in our town. It seemed romantic to me, a sixteen-year-old, falling madly in love, like in the movies, with a good-looking guy who loved to dance and sing in an off-key voice along with the music of the "Big Band" sounds of that era. Ed was my first boyfriend, and it was a special thrill showing him off to my high school friends when he stood waiting after classes, whistling jauntily on the steps, carrying my books, and walking me home.

97

When Ed asked me to marry him, I thought he meant when the war was over, so I said I would. Like thousands of other girls I'd write a daily letter, and after the war we'd settle down and raise a family. It was romantic dreaming on my part, but Ed was serious. He wanted to get married before his leave was over! He pulled a ring from his peacoat pocket and slipped it on my finger. I stammered that the ring was pretty, but I had to finish high school first. Yes, I would wear it, and we would be married right after the war. He conceded, smiling lopsidedly.

It was fun showing off my diamond at school and waving good-by to Ed from the railroad station, swept into the vibrant excitement of the mobs of people milling around watching the train pull away. The thought that we were too young nagged at the back of my mind, but my romantic dreams lulled my doubts into quietness. And after all, our marriage ceremony was far in the future.

How wrong I was! Right after I graduated, Ed wrote that we would be married on his next leave. I was to get ready. He was adamant. Hadn't he waited for me to finish high school? He would wait no longer. He needed hope, someone to come to, he wrote, if indeed he came home at all. Anyway, he would be stationed stateside, his letter said, and I could live on the base with him. Perhaps the strangeness of the times made me do something I would never have done in saner moments of history.

Ed and I were married three weeks after my high-school graduation, and we left for a weekend honeymoon. That's when he told me, a sly smile crossing his face, that actually he knew all along he had been assigned overseas and would be leaving the very next week. I felt tricked and deceived, and I had the sinking sensation that perhaps I had made the mistake of my life marrying a boy

98

I scarcely knew. I consoled myself with the thought that Ed loved me and couldn't bear the thought of losing me and had to lie so I would marry him.

Ed was stationed with a hospital unit on Okinawa when our troops were fighting to secure that island. He saw horrible things, cared for badly wounded men, agonized while his buddies screamed in pain as they lay dying, watched men with amputated limbs cry out in pain and despair, and perhaps right at that moment the seed of what was to come later was planted in Ed's vulnerable mind. He said it was seven months of "pure hell." Nightmares persisted in the years to come, and what should have become a dim memory remained vividly clear in Ed's mind.

War brides had been advised to be patient with returning veterans; with understanding and love the men would return to their normal selves. But I had lived with Ed only four months, and except for a mountain of letters hardly knew him at all. I was uncertain what his normal self was.

Somehow Ed needed to stop the tormenting memories of those months on Okinawa, and he turned to alcohol. In his drunken rages he cursed, lashing out at me; he was jealous of my time, robbing me of precious freedom like an ever-tightening vice. His hurt had been so great that the only respite seemed to be to inflict the same wounds on someone else, and because I was there I received the brunt of his anger.

There was restlessness everywhere during the post-war years. Jobs were scarce for returning veterans and apartments were difficult to find, forcing us to stay anywhere we could, with relatives or friends. After frantically searching, I found a one-bedroom apartment in the heart of the city close to public transportation, a necessity because we had no car.

Ed blurted out one day that he wanted me to have a baby, and when I became pregnant he changed overnight. He enrolled in night school and became solicitous and sensitive of my needs.

Chuckie was born after a long, difficult delivery, and I went home with firm orders that I must rest, an absurdity with a newborn baby, but I was so fatigued I could only rouse myself to care for the baby's needs and lay back in bed exhausted.

Ed was belligerently sarcastic. "You're not sick!" he would yell. "You only want sympathy, but you're not getting any from me. I've seen real pain. You should have been on Okinawa and then you'd know what real suffering is." Then he would go into minute detail about the men who had been burned and injured, how he had watched them die. Remembering his feelings of helplessness, he burst into tears. I knew his memories were still sharp, his suffering intense, but so was mine, and I couldn't relate to a far-off battlefield. My war zone was right there in that bed fighting to regain strength. My baby needed me, and that was primary in my mind.

Before Chuck was out of diapers I was pregnant again, plunging my spirits to a new low. We hardly had room in the cramped apartment for the three of us; bills from Chuck's birth and my long hospitalization were still unpaid. We had no car, not even a washing machine.

Ed was terribly disappointed in our second son, Jimmy, for reasons unknown to me. Even though Jimmy was bright and healthy, Ed refused to pick him up and practically ignored his presence, concentrating only on Chuck. Jimmy sensed this rejection and would cry the minute Ed entered the room, adding turmoil to the mounting frustration. Ed's unreasonableness was heightened by our small living space, but he had found greener pastures, a place of refuge. Right after dinner he headed for the corner bar, coming home long after midnight. Weekends were worse! Then he was with his friends doing whatever they did from morning until night. The telephone was my only link with the outside world.

When Congress passed a bill that veterans could purchase homes with no down payment, we became excited about owning our own home, but to my great disappointment Ed bought a house without consulting me. "You want a house, don't you?" he yelled. "Then you'll take the one I pick out." I blinked away tears, convincing myself that Ed would change once we moved into our own place, and for awhile he did seem content.

But slowly and subtly he became restless once more, and now I was his target. Nothing I did was right. The way I wore my hair, my choice of clothes; I didn't sweep the floor right or wash dishes fast enough. My eyes weren't the right color or I wasn't tall enough. His restlessness had only deepened, encompassing the whole world. Couldn't I see how unfair life was to him?

I knew our marriage was deteriorating and that I must get relief; self-preservation and the happiness of my children depended on it. But one morning when I awakened with the familiar nausea signaling another pregnancy, my plans of leaving Ed were forgotten.

Of all things, now he began accusing me of having an affair while he was working, a soothing of his own conscience I suspect, because one night he didn't come home from work. I was frantic and called the Highway Patrol. When the telephone rang around one-thirty in the morning, I was relieved, sure it was Ed with a reasonable explanation.

101

"Hello, Ed?"

"No, this isn't Ed," a woman's harsh voice said, "and what is your husband doing with my daughter at this hour of the morning?"

I replaced the receiver with a pounding heart, and while tears streamed a salty taste into my mouth I packed Ed's clothes and left them on the porch with a note asking him please to leave and never come back.

I waited for the sound of Ed's car and stiffened with tension when he turned the key in the lock. I met him at the door, angry but coldly calm. "Get out," I said. "If you have no more respect for me than to cheat and lie, you don't deserve a wife and two wonderful children. I don't want anything from you except a promise to never come here again."

Once more Ed turned on his humble charm, contritely begging my forgiveness, assuring me he would be different.

"Please give me another chance and you'll never regret it," he wept, and the ice in my heart melted.

We talked long into the night, communicating as we never had before, and Ed agreed we must work together for a life of happiness. But didn't I see that it was the war that had unsettled him? he asked. Now he realized how much his family meant to him, and he would change.

Year followed year, five in all, and Ed seemed to be the boy I had married—fun-loving, industrious, kind to me and the children.

We had two more children. A daughter, Nancy, and then Debby, born two years after Nancy. With four children under six, life was a whirl of diapers, runny noses, and running children. Ed insisted we didn't need friends; our little family was enough. I nodded, careful not to tip the scales again, fearful of making Ed angry and restless. Someday, I decided silently, he would gain self-confidence and trust in people, but for now I would be content with my family.

Maybe it was because of the pressure of Ed's new promotion on the job, but suddenly, without warning, ominous symptoms began to send fear trickling into my bones.

The first sign that all was not well with Ed came on a lovely Sunday afternoon drive through winding mountain roads. Abruptly Ed pushed the accelerator to sixty, seventy, eighty miles an hour until he was driving at breakneck speed through the hazardous canyon roads.

"Ed," I deliberately kept my voice steady, "we can't enjoy the scenery when you are driving this fast. Please slow down."

He looked at me in surprise as though that were a remarkable bit of insight and eased his foot off the gas pedal. Once again he was driving the thirty-five-mile speed limit, smiling pleasantly at the beautiful view on either side of the road. After that Ed never again exceeded thirty-five miles an hour no matter what the zone was.

His attitude toward the children shifted again, demanding more from them than they could possibly give.

"They're going to face a cold, hard world out there. They may as well learn to cope with it right now," he insisted.

What came next almost defies description. Ed became obsessed! First it was the space program which demanded he write lengthy letters to government officials explaining his magnificent theories and solving mathematical problems. When disinterested or negative responses

103

came, he raged against their stupidity and ignorance.

Next he purchased an expensive telescope, spending hours searching for UFOs which he "knew" were enemy aliens ready to take over our unsuspecting planet. Somehow, he raved, he would prove his theories were right, and if the government wouldn't finance him he would have to do it himself.

How, I wondered, looking around at our meagerly furnished house, the children's threadbare clothes, and the barest of necessities in the kitchen cupboard?

"There's a way," Ed said excitedly, withdrawing all the funds from our small bank account. "I'll double it, you'll see."

I saw, and my heart plunged. Ed lost it all at the racetrack and continued to gamble his paycheck every week until there wasn't enough money for our basic needs.

"They" were out to get him, Ed told me in whispers, laying rigidly in bed, and when I tensely asked who "they" were, the look in his eyes turned my blood cold.

It was too much for Ed: the rejection of his scientific theories, the loss of money, the imagined persecution from "them." He awakened morning after morning too ill to go to work, bewildered and nauseous, refusing to eat anything but junk food, lighting up one cigarette after another, drinking cup after cup of hot coffee sweetened with too much sugar.

The fear that had begun as a trickle was now a raging flood. Ed was deteriorating into a paranoid person.

"Did you hear that?" he'd whisper. "You're doing this to me. You know who it is and won't tell me." Running from room to room he looked behind furniture, turning chairs over, looking wildly under the bed, searching for something that wasn't there.

One terror-filled night in his search for "them" he was sure he had found the haunting voices. They were coming from the television set. Ranting and fuming he ripped away tubes and wires, throwing them wildly across the room until the back of the set was an empty shell.

"That will show them they can't get me," he smirked with satisfaction.

I phoned our family doctor who suggested a psychologist. Ed agreed to go if he could drive so the "voices" could lead him, which resulted in a circuitous route to the doctor's office.

The psychologist wanted Ed under surveillance for seventy-two hours, but informed me Ed should commit himself. He must want treatment and would respond more quickly if it was his decision.

"No," Ed shook his head, "I won't go to a hospital."

How can I describe the days that followed? It is even a jumble in my own mind. I remember Ed holding his head and alternately laughing, crying, and screaming at the "voices." Finally he reached for a bottle of whiskey to drown out the horror in his mind.

I counted the days, the minutes until our next consultation with the doctor, but when we arrived at his office we were told he was on vacation. Another psychologist would see Ed.

That day Ed was on good behavior, acting perfectly normal, calmly sitting back to chat as though he and the doctor were buddies planning a fishing trip.

How strange mental illness is! Ed, so wildly insane during dark nights, became "normal" on certain days until a particular subject triggered him into paranoia.

Today, dressed in a business suit, chatting with the doctor, Ed was adjusting his pretending mask.

The doctor smiled patronizingly at me. "I don't find

any signs of mental illness here," he said. "There's no need for hospitalization." Ed grinned at me, and I knew I had a real fight on my hands to get help for him.

I could cope during the day, busily keeping occupied with the children, tensing myself to ignore Ed's silent presence in the rocking chair. It was the nights that were filled with terror.

"Please, Ed," I begged," let's go to the VA hospital."

A silent stare, perhaps a wooden walk to the door, only to turn quickly back to his constant rocking.

One night Ed calmly told me that the voices had instructed him that we weren't really married. He was wedded to a celestial being. He and I must never have sexual relations again. And we didn't.

I clung to the memory of our few happy years and the hope the Ed would become what he had once been. He was definitely two people. One side of him was highly intelligent, spinning fascinating stories, delighting the children; the other side was filled with intense hatred, insecurity, and distrust.

Sleep was out of the question. Ed moved about the house restlessly, talking and mumbling, while I drifted in and out of the edge of sleep, deliberately staying awake, holding myself tensely in check.

One night when exhaustion pushed me into a deep sleep, I woke abruptly as surely as though someone had shaken me. Ed was moving about the kitchen, opening the drawers and examining our sharp knives, laying one down and holding up another, talking in loud tones. I walked into the kitchen and got a glass of water as calmly as I could.

"I'm thirsty," I forced myself to smile.

Ed stared back at me, put the knives in the drawer, closed it, and walked into our bedroom.

Weakly I sat down, scarcely noting the cold tiled floor beneath my feet. The chill of the room couldn't match the frozen feeling in my body. Outside the black window bare branches, swaying in the cold breeze, were outlined against a gray dawn. Stars were still high in the sky. In that stilled moment, trembling and frightened, one Name came to my mind forcing my head into my hands. "Oh, God, thank You for being here. I need You, wherever You are. Please help me."

Until this moment God had been a Presence, the Eternal Helper high on His throne. Who He was or how He related to me I didn't know, but I was certain the beautiful thoughts I had been taught in church were no longer sufficient. I needed a God who would be like a Father helping in my desperation. At that moment, with blackness thick in our home, a light went on in my soul. God was there calming my trembling and keeping my family safe.

That night was the apex of my terror. Never again could anything frighten me that badly—the horror of Ed holding those knives and looking through me without expression or recognition.

Doctors had failed me! Hospitals had failed me! I had to find One who would be faithful and caring, and that light in my soul turned on again. I needed to know God.

I had been sending the children to a small church a few blocks from our house, and each Sunday they came home as though a breath of fresh air had touched them, excited about what they had learned, gathering much-needed security from their friends and teachers. The following Sunday I went with them. It wasn't a beautiful sanctuary with gold crosses and stained-glass windows; in fact the group met in a gymnasium and sat on folding chairs. But from the moment I walked in and the music began to play, tears filled my eyes and refused to stop flowing. It was almost as though I had been on a far journey and had come home.

And that day I heard for the first time the saving words of the God I longed to know. I clung to them as though they were a life preserver in a stormy sea.

"All have sinned and come short of God's glorious ideal."

*Oh, yes, yes, how true!*

"God sent His Son, Jesus Christ, to the cross, His Lamb, that we might have forgiveness for our sin. He is the Savior of the world."

*How desperately I need a Savior.*

"Eternal life is available to you now. The Bible says 'As many as receive Christ, to them God gives the right to become the children of God.' "

*Yes, yes, Lord Jesus, I receive You.*

While the congregation sang the closing hymn, the Light of the World entered my life. I walked the long gym aisle, tears covering my face, aware that my children were beside me following that Light. That morning I was born anew!

I walked home gloriously happy, noticing the beautifully etched mountains in the distance, realizing they were clearly visible from my kitchen window, yet I had never really seen them because I was so bound in my fearful world. I almost skipped the last block home. But one look at Ed's face and the rude awakening struck me that this was a problem that had not vanished because I had found the Light of Life.

Things grew worse for Ed. The voices were almost constant now, and out of desperation I called his sister who came with her husband from the northern part of the state. By the time they arrived Ed had another obsession.

He declared himself to be Alpha and Omega and was fasting forty days and nights which only compounded the problem.

My brother-in-law took charge, and for the first time the load was shifted to someone else who cared. A gift from God! Ed was admitted to the VA hospital for a three-month period, then discharged as functional and sent home. Life became a nightmare again. The hospital became a revolving door. Four times Ed was admitted and four times was discharged in far worse condition.

Some of the time Ed wanted to be called "Schizzy" and sometimes Ed. One day he said he wanted to be called "Schizzy" all the time. That was the day I am sure Ed gave up the fight. He would no longer take medication or try to fight his illness.

But through it all my heavenly Father was faithfully by my side, supplying help through my new friends at the church. They were my "survival kit," offering prayer support, financial help, and unqualified love.

It had to end soon, the in-and-out-of-the-hospital routine, and one day quite unexpectedly it did. It was Saturday, and I was going to paint the front door. I put papers down in front of Ed, set the paint and can opener there, and asked him to open the can of paint while I scraped the door and removed the hardware. When I was ready to paint, Ed was still sitting in the same position, lighting up another cigarette and talking to the voices. His giggling stage had begun some time before and it was far more frightening than the rages or restlessness because it was so *insane*.

"Please, Ed," I insisted. "Open the can of paint."

He shook his head. "I've got a place where I can go and do nothing if I don't want to."

I spoke coolly, "Then perhaps you should go there."

"I don't see anything wrong with the way I am,"
he said. "I like being this way, not having to do anything.
Why can't you be more like me and let other people take
care of you. Welfare isn't that bad."

I stood silent, tears stinging my lashes.

Ed stood up, looked around the house, and announced
he was going back to the hospital. He never came home
again.

Science has yet to determine what causes schizo-
phrenia. Some doctors feel that a percentage of patients
can live rather normal lives or at least be functional by use
of medication. But many, like Ed, resist taking the drugs.

The social worker explained that the only way Ed would
receive permanent hospital care would be if I divorced
him. Though I didn't want to reject him, it seemed the
only answer. I waited two years before I finally filed. Now
Ed is in the hospital receiving the care he needs.

Families of mental patients have been unjustly blamed
for their loved ones condition. Along with everything else
there is to bear, this hurt goes deep into my soul.

Through all their formative years our children lived
with a mentally ill person. They have received psychiatric
care, but in the final analysis it was prayer that healed
our family. Our pastor and his wife spent many hours
counseling and praying that our souls would be
healed, our emotions restored, our subconscious minds
cleansed. Those prayers were our restorative therapy,
for the brokenness in our lives has been gloriously
healed and my children no longer need psychiatric
help.

Three years ago I remarried and now have the marriage
I dreamed about. Ron and I met at church, and we both
love Jesus Christ and seek to be obedient to Him. We feel
God brought us together as only God knew our

independent desires and could have worked it out so
beautifully.

For those still on that long heartbreaking road of mental
illness, I can offer a little of what I have learned.

Seek professional help early. Be careful in choosing
a therapist. Don't be afraid to interview the social
worker, psychologist, or psychiatrist so that you know
where they are coming from.

If you are a Christian, an unbeliever is not going to
be any help because their views will differ in every way
from yours, making you believe your principles are
foolish and confusing you even more.

Don't be afraid to admit to yourself and to others that
your loved one is mentally ill; minds can be broken
just like any other part of the body. Often people
would say Ed was acting like a spoiled child and could
snap out of it if he wanted to, refusing to believe he
needed help outside himself.

Hang on to your own identity.

Spend time with the Lord; read His Word; drink in His
love, care, and comfort.

Ask God to send a Christian friend to pray for and
with you.

Remember the words of Jesus: "I will never leave you
nor forsake you." You may feel forsaken by society,
but you will never be rejected by God who created
you and loves you dearly.

All My Tears

# 8 All My Tears

Sometimes we meet people who have suffered so much heartache that we wonder how they have survived as whole persons. Ruth's story gives us some insights into the "how" and the "Who."

*Ruth*

It was dusk. Dinner was over, and Ruth hurried about her small kitchen with an air of expectancy. The box of food was packed and in the refrigerator; all she had to do now was wait.

Her husband Paul was recuperating from the flu,

dozing on the sofa. She tiptoed into the living room and turned the TV set on low to watch the evening news. Every few minutes her eyes wandered to the clock above the mantel.

When the news was over, she sat restlessly through an old movie, struggling to keep the knot from tightening in her stomach. When Johnny Carson's face came on the screen, she turned to her husband.

"Honey, you go on to bed. I'll wait up for Tom and Patty."

He nodded sleepily, leaning over to kiss her.

"Be sure and wake me when they come no matter how late. I want to say good-by too." He looked at the clock. "Ruth, it's nearly midnight. They said they'd be here by ten. What could have happened?"

Ruth smiled softly at her husband. "It's okay. They may have been delayed saying good-by to Tom's relatives. They'll be here. I'll wait."

"Well, all right then. But be sure and wake me."

Ruth leaned her blonde head back and rocked gently. The clock was chiming twelve, and with each loud clang her spirits slipped further. Were they going to come at all? But Patty had assured her that very afternoon on the telephone that they would stop to say good-by.

What final hurting words from her only daughter just turned twenty-two. Patty and her young husband were moving three thousand miles away, fancying a dream life in California, the world of movie stars and fantasies. Lack of a job and unsure of a place to live didn't deter her headstrong daughter. True, Patty's own father George, was out there, but a lot of good he would be drinking and carrying on as he did.

Ruth rocked faster now, tears blinking through her lashes. She mustn't be crying when Patty came, but smiling, even laughing, clearing the air between them, breaking down the walls that had been built so high in the past few years.

She had carefully cooked chicken all afternoon, baked Patty's favorite cookies, tucked in lots of extra goodies so they could munch as they rode in their dilapidated Ford. She could hardly wait to hand the labor of love to her daughter and see her dark eyes widen in surprise.

Ruth stopped rocking and closed her eyes, reflecting back to Patty's birth and the thrill of holding her firstborn child. What a young and foolish girl she had been, getting pregnant before she was married, thinking her heady romance would last. Everyone had tried to warn her, but she had been blindly in love with George—teasing, laughing, handsome George so striking in his Navy uniform. He swept her off her feet, whispering that she was the prettiest girl in town, holding her so close when they danced she could almost taste the liquor on his breath. She didn't worry about his drinking; all men did that, even her father. She loved George, couldn't live without him, and once the baby was born he'd settle down. Everyone would see.

Looking back on her troubled past, Ruth didn't know where to place the blame. It wasn't her parents' fault; they were from the old country and couldn't understand American ways. Feeding and clothing their nine children was all they could handle. With dad's drinking and ma always pregnant, home had been a place to escape. But it wasn't her mother's fault either. One baby after another swelling her body—no wonder she harped at the older kids for help. She was weary, worn-out long before her time.

No, Ruth thought, it was her own fault for not trying to understand and stay with her mother after dad died, for wanting so much of the world she could feel it already in her grasp, for daring to think she could have a slice of the moon if she reached high enough, and for thinking George could ever be any part of her dream. He wasn't even a moonbeam or the tiniest reflection of the smallest star. He drank even heavier after their marriage, unable to resist pretty young faces, chasing after his own ellusive rainbow. After Patty was born, their son Georgie came quickly, and then George was shipped overseas, leaving behind a mountain of debts and not a cent of support money for herself and the children. There seemed nothing to do but file for divorce.

So there she was, barely nineteen, with two children to feed. She had no education, no skills, nothing but her youth and pretty face to keep her family together.

She began working nights in a bar, earning twenty-five dollars a week. Nothing was left after room and board were paid. The children wore hand-me-downs from her sisters kids or clothes from the Salvation Army. She desperately wished for something better for herself and the children.

When her mother died after a prolonged illness, guilt edged into Ruth's mind rebuking her that she hadn't cared more for her aging mother in spite of her own problems. Now her mother was gone and there was another void in Ruth's life.

One thing she had done; she made sure her children attended Sunday school, rain or shine. They learned about Jesus just as she had as a child. One day they both told her they had asked Jesus into their hearts. Ruth hugged Patty and Georgie close. Back in her inner thoughts God was there, a waiting Presence, Someone to talk to and plead with for wisdom and strength just to put one foot in front of the other.

"Working in a bar is all I know, Lord," she would say, coming home at four in the morning, the smell of alcohol saturating her uniform. Falling wearily into bed, she thought someday it would be different. Someday she would find a good man, someone to care for her family.

But in the meantime her children were as scattered as her life. Five-year-old Georgie boarded out with the Lawtons, a wealthy family who loved her son, showered him with gifts, and took him to fancy restaurants in their long black Chrysler.

Patty was another story; she was moved from one foster home to another, each family complaining she was too much to handle.

"Please make a better life for my children, God," she pleaded, and when the Lawtons called to ask with warmth and concern if they could adopt Georgie, it seemed a direct answer to her prayer. They invited her to their beautiful home in a fashionable section of town, explaining about all they could offer Georgie: the best school, clothes, and travel.

Ruth sat like an empty shell, crying and nodding, knowing Georgie would be better off in a real home with both a mother and father. So she said, yes, they could have her boy, but there was one thing, one very important thing: They must *promise*, now this was what mattered the most, they must *promise* he would be raised as a Christian. The Lawtons smiled, patted her hand, and promised. So Ruth went to court, riding with the Lawtons and Georgie, and signed the adoption papers with eyes so wet she couldn't see her own signature.

She held Georgie tightly, kissing him until his face was wet and salty from her tears. "I love you, honey, I love you, and someday you'll understand why mommy has to leave you now."

Georgie followed the Lawtons to their car, rubbing hard at his eyes, looking back at his mother with childish longing, not understanding at all. Ruth stood without moving until the big car was out of sight.

She'd get to see him, of course she would, they told her benevolently, and one day they did bring Georgie to her apartment while she was at work. The next day the telephone rang at the bar.

"I went to your house, mom," her son's childish voice explained. "You weren't there. Why can't I come home and live with you?"

Fighting for control, Ruth answered, "Because, Georgie, I have to work, and no one would be at home to care for you."

"But, mom," he pleaded, "I don't mind being alone. I could walk around the house until you got home, and then I would . . . I'd make your coffee," he added quickly as though he had mentioned a magic word.

*Oh, Georgie, my poor little boy, it's too late. You're my flesh and blood but not mine at all. I've lost you.*

Sobs tore at her, shaking her fragile body. Her boss Harry held her, patting her back, offering her a drink, telling her to go home and rest, take the day off.

One day, and Ruth could remember the exact day, a friend told her that the Lawtons had no intention of letting Georgie grow up in a Christian home. They were professed atheists. The walls seemed to be caving in on her, the earth shaking, or was it just her world falling apart? She had sold her son, the son she loved so dearly, into a godless home. Poor and insignificant as she felt, a spark of fight ignited inside her: she must and would have her son back home. She talked to everyone about Georgie, and finally her boss advised her to see an attorney. She tried to explain to the lawyer why she had permitted her son to be adopted, searching for words that would make it clear that she had to have him back. He seemed interested, smiling and nodding, until she told him who had adopted Georgie. He sobered quickly.

"It would take a better lawyer than I am," he said, fumbling with papers on his desk. "Mrs. Lawton's father is the judge of this court. You'd better find yourself a real smart attorney from the big city."

It was raining when Ruth left his office, a steady downpour that matched her dreary mood. How could she afford to hire a good attorney? And if she could, would there be one willing to fight against the powerful Lawtons?

During the next months Ruth began to suffer mentally and physically until she could no longer ignore the mysterious symptoms that were plaguing her. After a visit to the doctor and with his advice ringing in her ears, she went to a clinic in Canada where extensive tests brought a verdict of diabetes insipidus. She would need injections the rest of her life to keep her alive.

"Did something happen to give you a shock of some kind?" the doctor asked, and Ruth wept for her son.

Leaving the clinic with prescriptions and instructions on how to give herself the shots, Ruth was anxious for the blessed busyness of work. She began noticing a tall, good-looking man coming into the bar every night. His name was Frank, and one night he asked her to dance, invited her to dinner, and seemed interested in her troubles about Georgie and her growing problems with Patty's defiant attitude.

She remembered Patty as a little girl, dark-haired like George, promising to be a beauty. Patty as a teen-ager was something to look at: petite and shapely with shining dark hair and eyes that danced vivaciously. Coming to the bar where Ruth worked, perching on a stool, looking like she was twenty-five instead of fifteen, she laughed at the passes the men made and looked at her mother tauntingly. Ruth fought back a rising fear as she saw Patty's glassy eyes.

"You're taking drugs" she accused.

"Yeah, mom, yeah. Everybody takes drugs. It's no big deal."

"Everybody doesn't." Ruth began to cry, "Patty, you'll ruin your mind, your body, your beauty."

But Patty turned her off, lost on her own trip, and Ruth couldn't reach her daughter with words.

Drugs! All kinds! LSD, brilliant lights, fantasies, horrible flashbacks, nightmares, running for more, a silver tray loaded with a trip to any place she wanted to go. Up, up and away, Patty went where she didn't have to worry or plan, demanding a larger tray with a bigger spoon to satisfy her growing need.

Ruth saw and wept privately, adding Patty's troubles to her already broken heart. And Ruth wondered, edges of guilt gilding her, if Patty's rebellion had started because of what happened with Georgie.

Actually it was Patty who urged Ruth to marry Frank—Patty, who was living with foster parents, was anxious for a home and wanted a father like her friends. Ruth hid the growing sensation that she didn't, couldn't love Frank even though she knew he would be good to her and Patty. But the marriage was wrong from the beginning. Ruth's thoughts and emotions were totally involved with the son she had lost; her empty arms couldn't receive love until they held her little boy once more. She couldn't explain it, but there was a barrier between her and Frank. It wasn't enough that he had given her a home so she could have Patty with them; she wanted and needed Georgie, and her thoughts were consumed by him. An added problem was Frank's insistence that she quit working at the bar. She couldn't, wouldn't. She needed the independence and money of her own to set aside to fight for her son.

One day Mrs. Lawton called to tell Ruth that they were leaving to live in Germany. Would she like to see Georgie before they left?

For several seconds Ruth struggled for the right words. No, no, she couldn't see him, she explained to the voice on the other end of the wire; she'd never be able to stand the parting. She gripped the receiver hard and said clearly, "Mrs. Lawton, you made a promise you never had any intention of keeping. You promised that my son would be raised in a Christian home. You have not kept that promise, and I want him back."

The voice was chilly, ignoring her statement and asking Ruth again if she wanted to see Georgie one more time. It might be years before they returned to the States.

"Mrs. Lawton," Ruth said, "I *will* have my son back. The Lord God whom you deny will give him back to me. I won't have to go to court or pay any money or struggle or have any help from outsiders. One day my boy will come back to me."

Ruth turned away from the phone calmly. She didn't know where she had gotten the strength to say those words with such assurance, but she *knew* what she had spoken was true. She had knelt by the rocker, the same one she was sitting in tonight, and prayed, "I know I haven't paid much attention to You, Lord, but if You'll just let me have Georgie back, I'll promise You anything. Please, dear God. The lawyers say it would take a miracle. Well, okay, You're the One who works miracles. You see now I have a husband and home. I could take care of him." She continued to bargain while she waited on tables in the bar, mixing drinks, promising she would quit working if Georgie came home.

Ruth's sobbing cries were heard by God, and He began to work in His own way. In Germany, the Lawtons were frantic over Georgie's poor behavior and failing school work. His health was fragile, and he was overtly hostile.

They hired a psychiatrist to live in with them for a time and analyze Georgie, to discover where the problem lay. At the end of three days the doctor sat down with the Lawtons and said earnestly, "There's nothing wrong with this boy that his own mother can't take care of. He knows he has a mother and sister and can't understand why he isn't living with them. He feels total rejection."

The atheistic Lawtons were being manuevered by almighty God. They cut their ties in Germany and made plans to move back to the States. They wrote Ruth asking if Georgie could visit her when they returned.

Ruth jubilantly waved the letter before Frank, hugging Patty tightly. "Georgie's coming home. My boy is coming home."

"Now, Ruth, don't get your hopes up," Frank warned. But she knew God was answering her prayers; without a struggle on her part she was going to have her son back.

There was only one problem. Her marriage to Frank was ending, and a divorce was the last thing she needed if she wanted Georgie back. Frank had been understanding about her longing for Georgie, had tolerated Patty's rebellion and defiance, but Ruth had no love at all to give him back.

"I'll stay until you know what will happen with Georgie," Frank said, and Ruth was grateful for his gesture of compassion.

The Lawtons arrived in town and called Ruth to

invite her to dinner. Yes, Georgie would be there too. In fact, when the Lawtons came to pick her up, it was Georgie who came to the door for her. After nearly seven years Ruth was seeing her son face-to-face. She drew her tall twelve-year-old boy into the living room.

"Please sit down," she said swallowing the lump in her throat. "I have to finish combing my hair." She stood weakly before the mirror, tears begging to flow, her trembling hands holding her head. When she looked up, Georgie's reflection was beside hers in the mirror.

She turned.

"You know, mom," he said hesitantly, "I can stay with you if you want me."

*If I want you! Oh, Georgie, if you only knew!*

"We'll have to wait and see about the Lawtons, honey," she whispered.

At the dinner table over dessert Mr. Lawton cleared his throat. "You know why we're here, Ruth. We'd like to know if you want to readopt Georgie." Then they told her about the psychiatrist in Germany. Ruth listened with growing wonder at how God had accomplished His purpose without the smallest struggle on her part.

Georgie was looking at her questioningly. Ruth smiled directly at him. "Yes, yes, I want my son home with me."

And Georgie came home to his mother.

Frank left after the final adoption papers were signed, so Ruth was alone again, but now she had her children. And if she could help it, she would never let them out of her sight again.

One evening two years later Ruth met Paul, and when his arms went around her she felt she had come home. Now she could receive and give love freely.

They were married after Ruth was certain Paul loved her children. Georgie had never known his own father, had not related to Mr. Lawton, but was drawn to Paul, readily calling him "dad."

Paul and Ruth bought a little house in the suburbs, and for the first time Ruth could stay home and be a housewife. She loved that word, rolling it around in her thoughts while she cooked and baked and spent long hours in the garden. They were happy years with Georgie growing to be a fine young man.

But it was too late for Patty! She had built walls around herself that were too high to scale. She quit school and worked as a car hop. Pregnant before she was seventeen, she married Tom, who was even younger than she was. And always now there were drugs—from marijuana to LSD, she ran the gamut. Anything that would make her high.

Ruth had hoped that when Craig was born Patty and Tom would settle down, but Patty placed that sweet little boy in his grandmother's arms and ran off in search of more adventure. Their lives were headed for disaster, and Ruth could see far enough down the road to recognize the danger. Any warnings she offered Patty were met with hostility and contempt, building more walls between them.

Their latest escapade was this trip to California. Craig could stay with Tom's mother until they were settled, Patty reasoned, making it sound like a trip to the supermarket. It was, after all, the era of the sixties, the "do your own thing" generation.

Now the clock struck two. Ruth roused from her memories and paced to the kitchen window, separated the organdy curtains to look out, opened the front door and walked into the dark night straining to see if Tom's blue Ford was coming down the street.

She turned back and lay on the sofa, pulling the

crocheted afghan around her. If they rang the bell she could hear them, but she wouldn't go to bed until they came. But she could fight sleep no longer, and when she awakened it was morning.

Ruth never saw Patty again.

One postcard came from Las Vegas. "Mom, we came to say good-by at midnight, but no one answered the door." Ruth read that card over and over, agonizing over the message, asking Paul again and again if he had heard the door, but he shook his head. Had they come and knocked and she didn't hear? Or was Patty making up a story to please her mother? Ruth would never know.

When a note finally came from Patty, Ruth read each word carefully trying to find a clue to Patty's life style. She knew without being told that Patty and Tom were deep in the drug scene. She shivered to think what it must be doing to their minds and bodies. And all the time she prayed: "Lord, You brought my son back. Please bring my daughter home."

One balmy April evening Ruth was celebrating her birthday with her family. When the telephone rang, the brief thought crossed her mind it might be Patty calling to wish her a happy birthday. She never had before, but maybe this one time she had remembered. Paul answered the phone, and a puzzled look crossed his face. As Ruth walked toward him, he motioned for her to sit down. He was listening intently, and when the word "killed" slipped from his mouth the room began to whirl and sharp pains jabbed at her chest.

Paul held her tightly after he replaced the receiver, looking over her head to the stunned family standing beside the freshly cut birthday cake.

"It's Patty," he said. "She's been stabbed and shot . . . she's . . . she's dead."

Ruth tried to open her mouth to speak, but no words came. And when she heard peculiar high-pitched sounds coming from somewhere she realized they were screams from her own mouth. "Was it Tom? Did he kill Patty?"

Paul shook his head. "That was George, Patty's father," he explained. "Patty had been in touch with him and had his telephone number in her room. The police called him. A boy high on drugs stabbed and shot Patty. George says that Tom and Patty have been separated for some time."

"I have to go to her . . . I mean to California," Ruth said quickly, and Paul agreed, calling the airlines while her sister made arrangements to travel with her.

"I don't know why I want the airplane to go faster," she said as the giant bird winged its way west. "It doesn't matter if we're late does it?" And she sobbed, not caring that the other passengers were staring. Finally exhausted, she dozed, waking with a start remembering Paul's words, "Patty's been stabbed and shot."

Ruth wept, "Why, God, why? You brought my son back. Why did You take my daughter?"

"Did Patty come to the door that night?" she asked her sister, who couldn't possibly know. "Paul said she was crying out when she was shot. Oh, sis, maybe she called out for Jesus, do you think?" And she sobbed more tears from a broken heart.

She remembered her anguished prayers to God to bring Patty home. Maybe He had answered in the most merciful way for Patty and taken her Home to be with Him. A small comfort eased the penetrating sorrow.

In Patty's blood-soaked pocket was a letter written to a friend back home telling how she was tired of her life in California, wanted out of the drug scene, but she knew more than she should about illegal drugs and pushers and felt her life was in danger.

The funeral was small. Tom was there, sadly eyeing the coffin. And there was George in the corner, hardly recognizable, no longer the handsome young sailor she had once loved. Now he was a middle-aged alcoholic. He had never known his daughter well, and he didn't know his son at all.

Ruth and her sister drove directly from the funeral to the airport. Ruth couldn't wait to get home and feel Paul's arms around her. She had something she wanted to tell him.

"Paul, I promised the Lord if He got my boy back I'd live for Him. I didn't keep that promise, but now I must. I have to do something with my life so I don't feel like such a failure. I have to start all over. Will you go with me to talk to a minister?"

Paul agreed. They went together, and Ruth's broken heart began the healing process at the wise minister's counsel.

"God majors in failures," he said. "But He knows how to restore the lost years, erasing them from His memory, forgiving our sins and failures. He can make something good come out of suffering."

"But I'm so unworthy," she sobbed.

"Yes, Ruth, you are, and so am I, and so is the whole world. But God is love, and the measure of His love is total forgiveness. Don't let Satan bring up the past sin to condemn you. When God says He forgives, He does. And forgets. And restores."

Ruth hugged those promises closely. With the healing of her emotions came restored health to her body.

"A miracle," the doctor said.

"Yes," Ruth smiled.

Today Ruth is a caring, compassionate woman. A Martha—quick to serve.

Soft tears of understanding fill her eyes at another's sorrows as she remembers the years of her own heartbreak.

"God worked a miracle when it seemed impossible that I'd ever see my son again. I believe He met my girl when she was crying out and reached to her as she was reaching for Him."

Faith and trust are important words to Ruth, intermingled often in her conversation.

"Faith's eyes don't always know the reason *why*," she will say, "and faith and trust do not *need* to know. All my tears are collected and preserved in God's bottle, recorded in His book (Ps. 56:8). But now there is no looking back. Paul and I need guidance for the years ahead, and we have a verse that is our daily prayer: " 'Trust in the Lord with all your heart, and lean not on your own understanding; in all your ways acknowledge him, and he will make your paths straight' " (Prov. 3:5, 6).

Empty
Arms

# 9 Empty Arms

While waiting for a prescription recently at a medical building pharmacy, I noticed a line of teen-agers in front of one of the offices. When I wondered aloud what they were doing there, the pharmacist informed me they were waiting to sign up for abortions at a nearby hospital.

The young girls in faded blue jeans were laughing and chatting together as though they were lined up outside a theater!

It is certainly no secret that teen-age pregnancies are epidemic. So are abortions!

Something shamefully whispered about in privacy ten

or twenty years ago is now blatantly discussed over coffee. Appointments for abortions are made as casually as a six-month dental check-up.

In a television documentary concerning teen-age pregnancies, a seventeen-year-old boy told why he thinks teen-age pregnancy is so prevalent: "For one thing, we don't think it will happen to us. The other problem is peer pressure. We feel almost an obligation to sleep with a girl. It's like I got to go out and get me a girl to have sex with."

Another contributing factor to the epidemic of children having children is the crumbling of the family unit.

Every year thousands of teen-age girls, those who do not have abortions, bear children alone, the greater majority of them without benefit of caring parents or husbands. Giving the baby up for adoption seems the kindest option for both mother and child, yet with much pain is a baby taken from its mother's arms.

Trudy told me about the agony of this pain when I met her at a weekend seminar where I was speaking on the subject of "Coping with Heartache and Grief."

### Trudy

I gave up my baby.

My pregnancy wasn't the result of a love affair. I was raped. He was a boy I had dated and broken off with, so I suppose he didn't consider it rape but a kind of revenge. My inner self was violated, the part of me I thought no one could ever touch. After he left, I lay bruised, angry, and horribly degraded, weeping from hurt and frustration.

I honestly didn't think about the possibility of pregnancy until weeks later when I woke up one morning nauseous and dizzy, too sick to go to work. I broke into a cold sweat when I realized I was going to have a baby, *his* baby.

At first I hated him with an uncontrollable rage; then I despised myself for having dated him against everyone's warnings; and finally my anger turned inward toward the baby. I didn't have a good relationship with my parents so I couldn't go home, and I didn't want to involve them anyway.

I knew I couldn't, wouldn't take a human life. For me, abortion was wrong. So I decided to put my baby up for adoption.

But as the months went by, my anger turned into pity for this child who would never know his natural father and mother. The decision I had made would affect him for all of his lifetime. It wasn't a matter of copping out or ignoring the problem because the problem was inside me and would continue to be there for nine months. My only question was what would be right and fair for my child.

I was terribly depressed, lying awake at night wondering where to turn. My roommate helped me through that awful time in a way I can never repay.

It didn't seem possible that it was happening to me. I was in the pit of depression.

At the end of my pregnancy I found myself praying to God for wisdom. Falteringly I was taking steps toward Him. I had been away from Him for so long, but in the cumbersome months of waiting He was my only comfort. I came to the end of *me*, of my "trying tos," and helplessly gave myself and my baby to the Lord.

When my time came to deliver, my roommate went with me; she stayed with me the whole time during labor. Finally I was wheeled into delivery and soon I heard the nurse say, "It's a little boy, a perfect little boy." I heard a baby's cry so I turned my head in that direction, and I could see a little hand flailing over the top of a hospital crib. That was all I ever saw of my son. When I asked to see him, they just said 'Later, later,'' and wheeled me out of delivery to my room.

No one came to see me but my roommate, and as it happened, I was the only one in that section of the small hospital. I wanted to talk to someone, but I felt so ashamed I didn't know who to call.

One day the lady from the adoption agency came and said they would be taking my baby that day. They wouldn't let me see him. "For my own good,'' they said.

"Please,'' I begged, "make sure he's placed in a Christian home.''

The nurse told me there was no guarantee what religion the people would be who took my baby. I cried for weeks wondering if I had done the right thing by giving away my little boy. If only I could believe that I'd see him in heaven, I could accept it, but I don't even know it he'll ever hear about the Lord. I can never see him to tell him, never have the chance to hold him and tell him I love him.

Whenever I see a little blond boy about his age I stare into his face thinking he looks just like I did when I was a child. Then I tell myself I'm dreaming and walk away with a heavy heart.

Some people tell me I made the ultimate sacrifice in giving up my child, but I think I gave away the greatest gift I could ever receive—my own baby.

I can do nothing to change the situation, but if only I knew my child was raised in a Christian home . . . if only. . . .''


Some say it is best for a mother *not* to see the child she will never raise; other sharply disagree saying it helps resolve grief if she holds her baby even for a day.

I wonder what Jenny would say. She held her baby for several days before she unwillingly relinquished her to adoptive parents.

## Jenny

I held my little girl. Yes, I held her in my arms against swollen, aching breasts filling up with milk that she would never need.

My body hurt from the long hours of labor and delivery, but a greater pain engulfed my heart. I had signed adoption papers, and a home was waiting for her. My own child, part of me and a boy I had thought I loved, was only a loan for three brief days. Tell the sun to stop shining, order the moon to offer no glow, then tell me to forget those three bittersweet days!

When the nurse carried my baby away that third evening, she promised I could see her once more in the morning. Sleep was out of the question that night as I mentally tried to rearrange my life to make room for a seven-pound-four-ounce baby girl. But everywhere I looked my thoughts were jammed, dead-ended with no possible exit. And even if I could have found a solution, it was too late. I had signed away my rights as her mother even before she was born.

Could I have taken my baby home and said, "Here, mom and dad, you are now grandparents. While you thought I was in California having a summer of fun and excitement, I was sitting in the Salvation Army Home for unwed mothers." Or, "Oh, by the way, I gave your grandchild away to someone I will never see again."

No, I would have to go home willowy and tanned as though I'd just spent the most fun-filled summer of my life out west with my friend Karen who was supposed to be with me. She would back me up, nodding and saying, "Yeah, we had a great time basking in the sun."

We had lied to my parents, telling them we were going to California to stay with Karen's aunt, to work awhile and see the sights. They were reluctant because they had never met Karen, and I made sure they didn't know her last name or have her telephone number. "I'll write you. Yes, I will. I'll be good, and I'll come home by Christmas. After all, I am eighteen," I added for a definite touch of independence.

It was ironic in a way. Here I was, former homecoming queen, the girl voted "most likely to succeed," swiftly becoming the girl most likely to die of desperation.

And where was Richie, the boy who had promised to love me eternally?

"Hey, Jen," he was even smiling when he said it, "you know I love you, but I can't deal with this." And he had split, taking off in his van for parts unknown.

What else was there for me to do? A good girl from a respectable family in a small town. The invented story of a summer in California seemed the kindest choice. When I called the home for unwed mothers and they said they would reserve me a place, that settled it.

But I grieved. First, Richie's unconcern chipped at my heart, edging it in bitterness. And then the lonely grief of giving up my baby was almost more than I could bear.

That last morning with my daughter came too soon. When the sun peeked over the horizon, my heart sank. Soon the bustling nurse would appear with a cheery, "Good morning, and how are all our little mothers today?"

I had decided on a name for my baby during that long sleepless night. She would be Deborah Anne. When the couple came for her, I could tell them she had a name.

I held Deborah Anne for her morning feeding, touching her soft skin, gently caressing her wisp of brown hair, and when she opened her eyes wide she looked directly at me.

It was noon when the nurse came to tell me the adoptive parents were waiting in the downstairs lobby. I swung out of bed, reaching for my robe, and followed her to the nursery.

"Please," I begged, "couldn't I carry her down there myself?" I had to see the couple who would raise my child.

The nurse was kind. She nodded and placed Deborah Anne in my arms, walking ahead of me with the baby's formula. I held my baby, silently watching the elevator drop quickly from floor to floor. When the doors opened, they were there—a tall man in a business suit and a pretty woman with kind brown eyes. I was thankful her eyes were brown like Deborah Anne's, and as we stood awkwardly in a circle, my arms still tightly around my baby, a flood of tears burst from my eyes and ran down my face. I tried to brush them away and still hold on to my baby.

"Now, Jenny, it's time," the nurse said, and though I clutched my baby even tighter, she wrenched her from my arms, and I felt as though she were tearing away part of my heart. The woman gazed down at Deborah Anne, held her closely, and then looked up at her tall husband who was watching her tenderly. They were both oblivious to my presence.

I turned away, and the nurse kindly guided me back to the elevator. My arms were still warm from holding Deborah Anne, my robe a little damp where she had been pressed against me.

Back in my room, I stood at the window looking down into the parking lot; the man and the woman were getting into their long expensive car with my baby. Suddenly I remembered I had forgotten to tell them her name. I rushed for the elevator, but the nurse gently reminded me they were probably gone.

"Oh, please," I pleaded, "tell them her name is Deborah Anne."

She nodded, looking down at her papers, but I knew it was useless. That couple probably had their own name picked out long ago.

I went back to Chicago in the dead of winter just before Christmas. "Too thin," my mother said, "but nothing home-cooking won't cure."

I chatted brightly about California, the bright lights of the Sunset Strip, movie stars, the San Diego Zoo, Disneyland, wonderful white beaches, and the beautiful sunsets over the Pacific on a summer evening.

In reality I had seen nothing except crowded streets in downtown Los Angeles, the blocks around the Salvation Army home, and the bus stations leading to and from the big city.

But I had come close to God during that time, too. We had prayer every morning in the chapel, and I remembered what I had learned as a child in Sunday school—that God loved me and forgave me, not keeping score of my sins. He could turn the circumstances of my life into good so that I could grow spiritually.

It took a little more time to forgive myself; actually I was harder on myself than God was on me.

Deborah Anne will be sixteen this December. She is a teen-ager now, growing up somewhere in California, maybe with sun-streaked blonde hair and wide brown eyes. I see her in every teen-age girl on the streets of

Chicago, which is ridiculous, isn't it?

Of course her name isn't Deborah Anne, but that's the name in my heart and the prayer on my lips.

Giving up a baby is a heart-rending decision, an avenue of no return.

But there is another side of the picture, and that is the waiting home with parents who offer love and emotional, financial, and spiritual support which the child might not otherwise have. There seems to be a special bond between adoptive parents and their chosen children.

I remember the day close friends of ours brought a baby girl into their home. The love reflected in their hearts overflowed into that child's life. Today she is grown, a well-adjusted adult. Perhaps if the weeping young mother can envision her baby in loving arms, her tears will be partially dried.

"The Lord is near to the brokenhearted, and saves those who are crushed in spirit" (Ps. 34:18 NASB).

A beautifully comforting balm for the Trudys and Jennys who have empty arms and remembering hearts.

The Lord is near!

# Where Are You Going Without Me?

## *Where Are You Going Without Me?*

Where are you going without me?
You know I can't make it alone.
Why did you choose this moment
To turn my heart to stone?

Our marriage may not have been perfect,
But what of the memories we share?
Memories only we cherish,
About which nobody else would care.

What do I do with those memories?
And what of my heart of stone? . . .
I pray as you leave without me,
And I am no longer alone.

# 10 Where Are You Going Without Me?

Today there is one heartache that seems to be touching every family in one way or another—the heartache of divorce.

## Julie

It was Sunday again, and Julie fought the rising feeling that this was going to be just like every other Sunday had been during the past six months. Tom would stay in bed as late as possible, turn a disinterested face while she dressed for church, eat his breakfast in silence, and reach for the sports page of the *Los Angeles Times*.

And she would plead, beg, and complain about having to take their five children to church alone, which he knew was not easy, since they were all under twelve.

"The pastor called last night and asked if the boys could bring their building blocks and help him at the morning service," Julie told Tom, drawing his attention away from the paper. He nodded reluctantly, anger written on his face. Hardly looking at the children, he walked outside and waited in their Chevy van without speaking a word.

The boys were especially boisterous this morning, excited about getting in front of the whole church to take part in the Sunday school program.

Julie stole a quick glance at Tom's face and tried to make light conversation about the cool May day and the light rain greening up their valley, but he remained tensely quiet. She glanced back at their large farm house and her heart lifted. It had been a real find, sitting on two precious acres in the dwindling land of rural southern California. There were fields for the children to romp through and a small barn for their animals.

She and Tom had been like teen-agers when they discovered it three years ago, driving through the hilly, winding roads on a Sunday afternoon. They decided right there that they must have it and excitedly made plans to modernize the old house and make it a showplace. They sanded floors until the hardwood shone like glass, and they covered the walls with cheery wallpaper. When it was finished, the house looked like a page from *Better Homes & Gardens*. Tom and Julie stood back with pride, ecstatic over their finished work.

So what had gone wrong? Why and where did the happiness slip out of their marriage? Why was Tom staying at work later each night? Why was he locked into his private thoughts, sitting silently before the television, staring off into space. He played with the boys reluctantly now, and hardly noticed the girls at all.

The girls were from Julie's first marriage, one that had ended tragically. An auto accident had claimed her husband's life, leaving Julie a widow at twenty-five.

She met Tom at a church social for singles, and from their first date they had begun falling in love easily. They were active in the singles class, meeting with other young couples and joining in socials and Bible studies.

After their marriage three babies came in quick succession. She had had no time to think about their dwindling communication. Decorating the old house had drawn them closer for a time, but even that came to an end when the furnishing was complete. Somewhere the joy had faded, detouring into unhappiness.

"Oh, dear Jesus," Julie prayed, "please help me understand. I don't know what's troubling Tom, but our marriage is going. I'm losing him."

Lunch was tense that day. Tom was restless, glancing at the clock, fidgeting with the car keys.

"I'm going to the office."

"But why on Sunday, Tom?" Julie asked. "Is something wrong?"

"Yes," Tom said, turning to open the door, "something is wrong. I'll tell you what it is when I get home."

Clouds drifted lazily across the clear blue sky, peacefully tranquil, quite in contrast to the storm gathering in Julie's heart. She stumbled back over her memories in an effort to find the cause, any reason for what she knew Tom would say. Her prayers became scattered, pleading for help to make it through the day.

She heard the rumble of the van at dusk, and when Tom opened the door she stood motionless waiting for him to

147

speak. Then he said it, "There's someone else—a girl at work. Someone I care a lot for."

Weak knees, stinging tears, raging disbelief.

"Maybe if we talk, Tommy." She slipped into his boyish name unexpectedly. "Who is she?"

"Her name is Susan. I didn't mean for it to happen. We had lunch a few times, and well—it went from there."

The dam burst! Angry words were flung across the room. Back and forth they bounced—hurting, hostile accusations. Suddenly she had to check her feelings, remembering that the children were in the house. She walked erectly to the door of the family room and called them for dinner. There they sat, watching their favorite Sunday night program, innocently thinking it was just another evening, unaware that their world had just fallen apart.

The night seemed interminably long; even after the children were in bed nothing more was said. She lay beside Tom in bed, knowing they were miles apart. She was thirty years old and her second marriage was ending, though not by choice. This new pain brought back the grief of her first husband's death, doubling the hurt.

She imagined Tom holding another girl, whispering sweet things that were once exclusively hers. She cried herself to sleep.

When she awakened in the morning, Tom was gone. Their words the night before seemed like a bad dream. She got the children ready for school, keeping conversation flowing until the door closed firmly behind them. Then she stood before the full-length mirror and examined the image looking back at her. A slightly upturned nose, wide blue eyes, clear skin with just the right tint of rosiness had made it possible for Julie to be a sought-after model before her first marriage. She still

148

wore a size five and her appearance hadn't changed, but now she felt ugly and unloved.

The sharp ring of the telephone jolted her back to reality, and when she heard a female voice on the other end she sat down quickly. It was *her.* Julie's hands began to tremble, her mouth turned to cotton.

"My name is Susan." she said. "Did Tom tell you about me?"

"Yes," Julie whispered.

"I'm sorry. We never intended this to happen. It seemed so innocent at the beginning. I'm a Christian, too, you know."

Julie listened to the voice repenting of wrong feelings but reaffirming that she and Tom couldn't give each other up. She waited until the voice finished a sentence, then she quietly hung up. She could think of nothing to say.

Tears of angry frustration raged down her face. How dared that woman call her and say with such ease that she was a follower of Christ, yet find it so simple to break His commandments?

"Lord," she prayed, "don't let me make things worse. Maybe Tom will get over her if I'm sweet and kind. I know I haven't been the kind of wife I should have been."

She told Tom that night, "Your girl friend called." He stood by the door restlessly, wanting to leave, but Julie asked if he would please sit down and listen. He did, at first on the edge of his chair. Finally he settled back and they were able to talk in a way they had not communicated in a year.

"I don't want to give up on our marriage, Tom," Julie said. "We have five children to think of."

"I don't think it will work," Tom said. "Even if there

weren't Susan. I'm just the kind of guy who needs my freedom."

Julie thought of the demanding mortgage payments, the loan on the new van Tom had insisted on buying, the high cost of raising five children, and she wanted to scream. Yes, it would be nice to be free, to walk away from it all! But she kept silent, nodding as though she understood that, yes, he must have his freedom.

"Will you stay for six weeks until the children are out of school?" she asked.

He nodded. *Six weeks!* She could win him back! She would be sweet and loving so that he'd never want to leave. She got up quickly and went to the kitchen to prepare dinner, letting her tears mingle with the potato peelings and fighting against a rising nausea.

The next day as stillness spread over the house she called her friend Cindy. When she heard Cindy's voice, she began to cry.

"I'll be right there, Julie," Cindy said, and within minutes was at the door.

"It's a nightmare!" she told her friend. "Nothing I did was right. I couldn't make Tom happy. I failed as a wife."

"Julie," Cindy reached for her hand," you can't change Tom. You can only change yourself, your feelings and attitudes. You are not responsible for his actions, only your reactions. You are not responsible for another person's happiness. That's too heavy a load to carry. Let God love you and speak to you through His Word."

"God is all I have now," she wept.

"And He is enough," Cindy promised.

The Bible became Julie's best friend, her comfort during long evenings when Tom didn't come home. She turned to the Psalms, tracing the words, reading with new understanding.

> *O God, have pity, for I am trusting you!*
> *I will hide beneath the shadow of your wings*
> *Until this storm is past (Ps. 57:1 LB).*

And:

> *I will extol the Lord at all times;*
> *his praise will always be on my lips. (Ps. 34:1).*

*Always?* How was it possible through dark days and nights and a future without Tom? Bless? The word had a soothing sound, and Julie said it aloud. "How can I praise and bless you, Lord, when I'm losing my husband to another woman?" Her inner heart heard the words once more, "at all times."

When the six weeks were nearly over, Julie knew without Tom saying it that the time had been a sentence, one he was glad was almost over. His marriage was a prison; ahead he envisioned freedom and carefree living.

At that point Julie had to lay down her bitterness, resentment, and anger. For even though Tom was a Christian, had prayed and worshiped with her, she could not judge him or wish judgment on him, leaving that with God who knew his heart and motives and worked in perfect timing.

One night her Bible was open to the Psalms, and as she read she suddenly realized where she had made the wrong turn in her marriage—in her life. She had depended on *Tom* for happiness, wanting him to fulfill her life when it was Christ alone who could satisfy. She had leaned on *Tom* for support when Christ had promised to be her Rock. She had expected *Tom* to be her security when only Jesus was Safety. No one, not even

Tom, could exclusively fill the deep need in her life. That was reserved for the Lord.

Tom left at the end of six weeks, packing quickly after the children were asleep. Julie sat quietly in her chair allowing the peace and comfort of the Holy Spirit to wrap warm arms around her, promising her that He would not leave or forsake her. The silence when Tom left seemed infinitely better than the tension when he had been at home.

In the morning she told the children what she could not say earlier.

"Dad's been having problems, and he's not going to live at home any more. He still loves you and always will, but this is how it has to be. God is going to take care of us."

The quiet of the following days brought fresh desperation when Julie realized she had to begin charting and planning her own life and the lives of her five children.

"I'll have to sell the house, get a job, take care of the kids. I can't—I can't do it," she sobbed to her friend Cindy.

"Don't think about that right now," Cindy comforted. "Try and live one day at a time, thanking God for each day you make it through. It will work for you because God promised 'As your days, so shall your strength be.'

"I've cried so many tears," Julie said. "I wonder when I'll stop."

That's when Cindy reminded Julie of a verse that would forever make the Psalms precious to her. It was a love letter directly to her heart:

*You have seen me tossing and turning through the night. You have collected all my tears and preserved them in*

*your bottle! You have recorded every one in your book"*
(Ps. 56:8 LB).

The incredible thought that the Lord God, the designer and creator of the universe, loved her so much that He collected and preserved her every tear turned Julie around, revealing God's love in a new way.

"I've been able to forgive Tom," she told Cindy a year later. "Whenever I talk to the children about their father, I mingle the name of Jesus so there will be a softness and love in my voice. And, of course, there is power in that Name to forgive and heal and love."

The "me first" philosophy of today's society has created a selfish generation immersed in materialism, searching for answers to fill the emptiness, rushing from movement to movement, from person to person still unsatisfied.

The aching reality are the children of divorce; the real victims, suffering a whirlpool of emotions expressed or unexpressed, many destined to repeat the same destructive pattern in their own lives.

I recall echoes of voices through the past years saying the same words. The names and faces were different but the feelings were the same: aloneness and heartache.

"He left me for another woman."

"I'm so alone. I never thought this could happen to me."

"After twenty years—I can't believe it."

"I thought we had a good marriage, that she loved me."

## Joan

Diapers, formulas, kindergarten, Little League, car pools, neighborhood get-togethers, housework, and waiting for Ken to come home late from his busy office with a bulging briefcase filled with papers that needed his urgent attention. All this had seemed enough for the first ten years of Joan's married life.

If a small rumble of discontentment was felt, Joan quickly suppressed it. After all, she was living in a lovely home, was married to an ambitious husband rapidly climbing the ladder of success, and had two fine children. What else could she possibly desire?

But the voice of the feminist movement speaking of lost identity, self-fulfillment, and woman's rights in society touched a responsive chord, and Joan began her restless search the year she turned thirty.

Somewhere along the way, time had slipped by as though she were standing still watching the days whirl past from her environmentally controlled existence. Romantic love was a thing of the past. Ken was jetting across the country doing productive, important things relating to the needs of the world while she stayed home, useless and unneeded. The children were growing up, busy in their own world. It seemed ludicrous that a woman with a degree in business management had accomplished nothing more than raising children, chauffeuring them around the city, cooking, cleaning and sitting alone in the evening in front of the TV screen, unseeing and uncaring.

She didn't know how it started. At first she was just attracted to Gary, Ken's best friend, because he had such a stimulating mind, such an intense way of looking at life, and she felt alive again when she talked to him over a cup of coffee when he happened to drop by during the day. Soon they were having lunch together in out-of-the-way places. Finally they were spending week-ends together when Ken was out of town. They

shared intimacies Joan once would have labeled
infidelity. Not now! This was different. This was a slice of
happiness that she deserved; the "what about me"
philosophy soothed her guilt, except during midnight
hours when she lay awake, wondering uneasily where
this affair with Gary would lead.

But when they were together she knew a need so great
to feel his arms around her, his low voice caressing
her with endearing words, assuring her that she was
the only woman he had ever loved. She became alive,
glowing; she slimmed down, and tinted her hair a
brighter shade of blond; she was a woman in love,
fulfilled.

One had to be an expert liar to carry on an affair, Joan
discovered, covering up for hours away from home,
avoiding the look in her children's trusting eyes, lying
rigidly in Ken's arms when he did reach for her.

There were no more contented moments anywhere.
It was an effort to enjoy even the smallest things at
home. Family barbecues around the swimming pool,
reading a book by the fireplace, or simply enjoying the
solitude of her house when the children were in school
seemed quiet pleasures of the past. Now her every
thought was consumed with Gary. What was he doing?
Would he call tomorrow? When would she see him again?
What were they going to *do*? She had to force herself to
listen to the children's chatter or concentrate on Ken or do
the slightest household chores.

And gradually, without knowing just when it
happened, the affair wasn't exciting or exhilarating any
more. It was tensely troubling, a roller coaster that
wouldn't stop, a merry-go-round endlessly whirling,
faster and faster, the riders gasping for breath, hanging
on tighter and tighter, going nowhere.

But they couldn't break it off either. All attempts at a final good-by became one more telephone call, one more meeting. Two unhappy, driven souls, Joan and Gary agonized over their hopeless plight, unable to do anything but meet furtively, choking down guilt, trying to convince each other that they were not at all like other couples involved in cheap and sordid affairs.

It had to end and it did, quite abruptly. Gary was offered an out-of-state transfer and accepted quickly. He told Joan about it over the telephone, saying he hated to leave, but . . . well . . it was a promotion and what could he do?

What indeed! Joan leaned against the wall after she hung up, weeping and struggling against feelings of weakness and disbelief. All the words they had spoken meant nothing, for she knew by the undertone of relief in his voice that she had been dropped—rejected.

She saw Gary once more, and he wouldn't meet her eyes, explaining that this job was a great opportunity for him, finally saying it would be better if they were separated because, after all, they both had families and Ken *was* his best friend.

She wanted to scream, to ask where his thoughts of Ken had been during their intimate moments, but keeping her dignity seemed most important. So she walked away, her head held high.

She fixed dinner that night in a daze, walking through the motions. For the first time in weeks Ken was home early, looking pretty grim himself.

After the children were in bed he said, "I want to talk to you—now."

Not tonight, her mind begged, not tonight when I've been cast aside, when my heart is open and wounded. But Ken took her arm and sat her firmly on the sofa.

"Something's been wrong for a long time, and I want to know what it is."

"Forget it, Ken. It's all over," Joan shrugged off his hold on her arm. He gripped her again.

"What's all over?"

"You've obviously suspected that something's been going on, and it has," she said coolly, no longer caring if he knew.

"With who?"

"I don't want you to know." Joan turned her eyes away from Ken's penetrating gaze.

"Then we'll sit here all night until you tell me." He sat across from her, arms folded, face set.

Weariness seeped into Joan's body. She closed her eyes, leaned her head back against the sofa, and said softly, "It's Gary."

Ken fell back as though she had hit him, staring at her a long time before tears came to his eyes and sobs shook his body. He cradled his head in his hands.

"How could you? I put you on a pedestal. I trusted you—"

"You put me on a pedestal?" Joan said, and her voice went out of control, bitterness biting through each sentence.

"That's not where I wanted to be. I'm a flesh-and-blood person. I wanted arms around me, not to be high and lifted up so I couldn't be touched or express my feelings. I wanted to be loved."

Ken wasn't listening. His face was hard. "I could kill both of you."

That night Joan lay next to her husband, taut and wide-awake, wondering if their marriage was over. She had lost Gary, and now Ken was deadly in his silence, lying on his side as far away as he could get. Tears slipped down her face during that long black night. Would she lose her home? Her children? She had jeopardized everything precious to her, and for what? A few empty words and arms that had no right to hold her.

Joan and Ken maintained a politely cool facade for the children's sake, but they became strangers living under the same roof. Ken stayed away from home more than ever, and Joan wondered if he had decided that what was good for the goose. . . . He was a good-looking man and worked with beautiful girls. After awhile she didn't have to wonder. He told her, flaunting his affairs before her, using words with double meanings in front of the children so that they could hear but not understand.

During the long lonely days, the silence in the house became a smothering thing. One day Joan turned on the stereo loud and blaring, deciding to clean the house in a kind of frenzy, scrubbing floors, washing windows, and cleaning kitchen cupboards until they were spotless. Chores that had been left unattended during her days of preoccupation with Gary were doubly demanding. Now she went on a rampage to restore her home to order as though she could redeem her failing marriage with a day of housecleaning.

She was finishing the last of the kitchen, perched high on a chair reaching into the back of the cupboards, when her hand fell on something soft and leathery. It was the Bible she had had in high school. She brought it out, holding it close while a torrent of tears rained down her face. A storehouse of memories of her childhood and teen years came tumbling back just by holding the book that had once been precious in her life.

During college Joan had laid aside Christian beliefs along with her Bible. The belief that God really cared about her personally, that He guided in small and large ways, that He was concerned about her cares, anxieties, and future plans seemed absurd, busy as He was managing the universe. Joan didn't think of God at all. He was obsolete, a figment of other generations; He was not for today, and surely not for her.

Now she stumbled off the chair, turned off the stereo, and sat in the living room weeping and cradling the Bible like a lost friend. She didn't remember when her tears turned to a prayer, a cry for forgiveness for sinning against God and Ken. The memories of her love for Sunday school came back and the name of Jesus fell from her lips. "The blood of Jesus Christ his [God's] Son cleanseth us from all sin" (1 John 1:7 KJV). How glib that verse had sounded when she memorized it as a child, but now the reality of the truth was clear: *only* His blood could cleanse and wash away the stain of her sin—even the memory of it.

As though through a transparent door, Joan saw herself, the resentment she had let build up in her life, the bitterness toward Ken for not spending more time with her,—all the "little" sins that had culminated in adultery. And as she confessed her sins one by one, the weight of guilt fell from her heart as effortlessly as her tears. She read David's psalm of repentance as though she herself had written the words:

> *Oh, wash me, cleanse me from this guilt.*
> *Let me be pure again.*
> *For I admit my shameful deed—it haunts me day and*
>   *night.*
> *It is against you and you alone I sinned, and did this*
>   *terrible thing. . . .*
> *Sprinkle me with the cleansing blood and I shall be clean*
>   *again.*
> *Wash me and I shall be whiter than snow. . . .*

> Don't keep looking at my sins—erase them from your
> sight.
> Create in me the new, clean heart, O God, filled with
> clean thoughts and right desires.
> Don't toss me aside, banished forever from your presence
> (Ps. 51:2–4, 7, 9–11 LB).

Forgiven!

Forgiven by God but not by Ken, who turned a cold face to her when she asked him to please forgive what she had done.

"Never, Joan," he said. "I'll forgive in time perhaps, but I'll never forget."

Forgiveness without forgetting was not forgiveness at all.

And yet, Joan was at peace now. Even with Ken staying away, refusing to look at her, talking in clipped sentences when he did communicate, she was at peace for the first time since she had turned away from God.

She had found her identity, not in another man's arms but in Christ who was eternal, faithful, assuring her that she was worthy to be accepted as His child.

Joan gave poured-out love from Christ to Ken, but if he noticed he didn't let it show.

And then Ken nearly lost his life. An accident tore up his face so badly it took several plastic surgeries to reconstruct the bones. Joan stayed by his bedside, tenderly caring for him through his long nights of pain and fear that he would never look the same, reassuring him that she loved him and that their life would begin anew. When her pastor came to visit, Ken asked for prayer, and Joan's spirits lifted.

The operations were successful, leaving only two small scars on Ken's handsome face. But the scars on his soul had not been healed, for when he came home he sat alone by the pool sunning himself, turning carefully away when Joan sat beside him on the lounge chair.

And suddenly Ken was wealthy. His father died, leaving him a considerable legacy of money and land. That's when he asked Joan for a divorce.

No, he wouldn't go for counseling, and it wasn't because of Gary. It was another woman, and he wanted a divorce. He also wanted the house, the furniture, and their teen-age son. He would give her a cash settlement and set her up in an apartment with their ten-year-old daughter, but there would be no reconciliation.

"Divorce is like death," Joan told a friend after she had moved into her two-bedroom apartment in the heart of the city. "I've been through all the stages of denial, shock, bargaining, and now at last acceptance. Through it all God has been very close. There's no doubt that I have reaped what I have sown, but Jesus walked through the reaping with me and that made all the difference."

"My deepest mourning came when I cleaned out the house to move. Memories of twenty years were stored everywhere. The paper plates from our wedding with our names 'Joan and Ken forever' printed on them, our family protrait, photo albums filled with snapshots of happier days, memories of our trips to Hawaii, Christmas decorations. It was like going to my own funeral."

"God hates divorce," she told another divorcee, "but it is not the unpardonable sin. When Jesus spoke to the woman taken in adultery, He didn't tell her to go and do this or that and then He might forgive her. He simply said, 'Go and leave your life of sin.' She was freely forgiven."

So is Joan! Now she readily shares God's secret that it is Christ in her, the hope of glory and fulfillment. "Happiness,'" she says, "is just a by product of peace."

Ken never forgave her, but how could he when he himself had never experienced God's great forgiving love? It takes a forgiven person to forgive.

What a contrast to the story of Ted and Sally and the forgiveness Sally could offer to her unfaithful husband because she herself knew the forgiving love of God.

## Sally

At first it was like dying a slow death when I knew Ted was with another woman. At the beginning anger consumed me, and I became so nauseous I couldn't eat for days. I'd put the children to bed at night, try and watch TV or read a book, but the chiming clock kept reminding me that Ted was with her. At the chime of twelve (those twelve chimes always seemed slower and louder) I'd start to cry. If I hadn't had the children, I would have tried to find him. I called bars, feeling shame and wondering what the bartender must think of me, the jealous wife checking on her husband.

The clock striking one was even worse, infuriating me so I'd start throwing things or else just stand in the middle of the room crying, forsaken and alone, just me and the walls.

One day I went to Ted's office unexpectedly and found them in each other's arms. I began to tremble and ran for the car, tears flooding my face.

That was the cruelest day of my life, and out of sheer frustration I sat at the table and began to write out my thoughts in great jarring sentences until I realized I was writing to God—a prayer of relinquishment, giving up all that I owned for His perfect peace.

I began to envision my home as an altar, and I gave my husband and children to God, promising the Lord that when Ted came home (or if he didn't) I would still see him on that altar. He was not my responsibility, but God's, since Ted was a believer, and I knew Jesus the Good Shepherd would bring him back.

Now I was freed to worship and adore the Lord. My verse? "Let him have all your worries and cares, for he is always thinking about you and watching everything that concerns you" (2 Peter 5:7 LB).

I didn't say anything more to Ted, didn't ask him where he was going or when he would be home, and soon the affair was over. During that time God did a work in my life. He showed me my failings, and I knew I had to forgive Ted as freely as God had forgiven me."

"Sally," I asked, "was it really that simple to forgive Ted?"

"It was only possible when I remembered," she answered.

"Remembered?"

"Yes, when I remembered how God had forgiven me. That I was commanded to love and that the true measure of my love would be my forgiveness."

"And of course remembering God's word, "Be kind and compassionate to one another, *forgiving each other, just as in Christ God forgave you*" (Eph. 4:32).

No Promise
of Tomorrow

# 11 No Promise of Tomorrow

Kathy Leonard and I were having lunch at the Black Swann Inn on a glorious spring day, the kind Midwesterners dream about during months of winter blizzards.

Kathy was a fun person with dancing blue eyes. She was the girl who brought the first hot meal when you were sick, the much-loved den mother, the driver in the car pool who didn't complain, joking with the piled-up kids in the back of her station wagon. There was no outward sign that she was a woman who had walked through the valley of heartache.

As Kathy and I enjoyed the beautiful day and a

delicious meal, she began to tell me about her walk through the fires of sorrow.

## Kathy

Don and I were in our late twenties. Life was ahead of us, full of promise, rich with the joy of married love and three beautiful children.

Everything was on course the way we had mapped it out through our dating years and early months of marriage. We had worked toward our goals with youthful energy, and everything had fallen into place exactly the way we had dreamed. Don had earned his Ph.D. and was offered the position of College Dean at Trinity College and Seminary in Deerfield, Illinois.

After years of pinching pennies while Don was going to school, it was heaven to settle down in our first home and begin what we called "real living." We had six blissful months before the blow fell.

Don had been overly tired, suffering with severe headaches. At first we put it down to the pressure on the new job, expecting that when he became more familiar with it the headaches would ease. But they didn't. So we made an appointment with the doctor who ran extensive tests.

When the doctor called us into his office, he sat uneasily at his desk, twirling a pencil in his hand, not meeting our eyes. Finally, gently and in terms we could understand, he told us. Don had leukemia. I wanted to scream "How long? How long does he have?" but the words wouldn't move past my frozen jaw.

When we walked outside a fresh winter storm was blowing in, but we didn't notice. The penetrating cold couldn't have made me shiver any more than

I already had from the bitter diagnosis.

Don drove with infinite care, concentrating on keeping the car steady on the icy roads. Snow was piling into drifts, blinding our view, matching my mood exactly, as though we were driving into darkness.

I took deep gulps of air, stealing a glance at Don't face. It was a time for silence, but the stillness in the car was voicing a multitude of things neither of us could put into words. Our carefully planned life was ending before it had even begun.

*O God, the children!* They were eight, six, and just over a year old, so young to lose their father. And then reality struck me—I, Kathy Melton, would be a widow before I was thirty years old. How could I provide and be a mother and father to three children? And what about Don? What must he be thinking having just been handed a death sentence?

I'll never know how I got through preparing dinner and putting the children to bed, but I did. After the house was quiet, Don lit the fireplace and silently held out his arms. I walked into them as the suppressed tears rained down my face. Don, as always the strong one, comforted me.

There was an emotion rising that I couldn't name. It went to bed with me, kept me awake while Don slept, made me stumble into the living room and stare out the window at the steadily falling snow. It was a choking sensation, gripping me tighter and tighter until each breath became labored and heavy. When I began to shake uncontrollably, I knew. It was FEAR!

Panic drove me to my knees, my Bible opened before me. Looking down through wet eyes, the words were a jumble of black print. But, underlined in red, these words almost jumped off the page:

> *Do not fear, for I am with you;*
> *Do not anxiously look about you, for I am your God.*
> *I will strengthen you, surely I will help you,*
> *Surely I will uphold you with My righteous right hand*
> (Isa. 41:10 NASB).

I poured out my fears to God, accompanied by my own muffled sobs and the sound of the winter wind. By the time I arose from my knees, the faint light of dawn was at the window and fear had loosened its grip on my body; and peace whispered that though the days ahead would be rough, I would not be alone. My God would be with me.

I slipped into bed and snuggled close to Don, feeling the warmth of his body, wondering what it would be like when his place beside me was empty, his pillow smooth and untouched.

The doctor answered the question which hung heavily on our hearts: How long? Six months, he said. *Six months!* It didn't seem possible that by next winter's snowfall Don would be gone. Denial took over as I refused to believe the awful truth. Doctors had been wrong before. Don and I would fight together against this horrible cancer invading his body, and we would win.

*Chemotherapy!* The side-effects of the treatment were worse than the disease. I pleaded and bargained with God for time, just a little more time, and suddenly that prayer was answered.

*Remission!* What a glorious sound for those caught in the awful trap of a wandering malignancy invading blood cells, running rampant throughout the body. My joy exceeded my reason! To me remission meant Don was healed. I pushed away the certainty that leukemia was a killer, a deadly disease irrespective of persons, even my husband.

Don, back at work, seemed healed, and in my joyous hopes I believed he was. But the clock was ticking away the days and hours, borrowing time, which for Don meant three years from the first diagnosis. Three *added*, memorable years together, joyous, filled-up days printing memories on our children's minds.

What words can describe the night I knew Don's time was nearly up? The night I caught the gray look of pain on Don's face. His eyes were closed, his head leaned wearily back against the sofa. I sat in the darkened kitchen trying to gather my pounding thoughts. It was black outdoors, staring through the windows like a thousand midnights; not a star was in the sky.

It seemed like the world was dying.

My world was!

I walked back into the den and nestled on Don's lap, clinging to him, not caring if my sobs were great and heaving, not bothering to fight back tears any more. Don cradled me gently, not shedding one tear. He passed what little strength he had left on to me.

The following morning I drove Don across icy streets to the large, formidable hospital on the edge of town. A wheelchair was waiting at the door, and as I followed as they wheeled Don to his room, I kept thinking, "The last mile."

We shared our last Christmas with Don as father and husband. Sitting by his bedside as the year was coming to an end, I felt hot tears sting my lashes and I allowed myself to grieve freely. *Oh, Don*, I whispered to the sleeping man lying so still, *I'll do my best. But, oh, I'm going to miss you—your strong arms around me, your*

*wise counsel when I need advice, the sound of your*
*voice.*

New Years Eve! The old year was fading into the past and so was Don's life. The world was dancing and celebrating, toasting the new year, while I sat quietly beside my husband, my love, holding his feverish hand. Before the clock struck midnight, Don slipped quietly into eternity.

Don's pain was over. He was Home.

I walked steadily to the telephone booth to call my parents, then stumbled back to a bench in the dark, silent corridor to wait for them. The children were staying with close friends. I would wait until morning to tell them their daddy was gone.

The waiting was over. No more pleading and bargaining for time. Time had run out.

Days faded into weeks, weeks into months; life flowed back into its natural pattern. Groceries needed to be purchased, meals cooked, houses cleaned, washing done, clothes folded. Children must go to school, must be chauffeured to their various activities, must be listened to. And one day I felt it: the hostility. It was directed at me as though I were the one responsible for their father's death. The two older children were grieving in their own way, resulting in problems at school or in neighborhood skirmishes. I needed Don, oh, so desperately, but his space was empty. He was gone!

God was silent! I had experienced His silences before, but now heaven seemed a sky of iron. So I did what I could; I leaned on the silence. Lying on the floor, my face wet with tears, I asked God to show me where to turn, what to do, how to manage my children.

It was a time to mourn, and I did!

As heartbreaking memories tore at my heart, I

remembered something Don had whispered to me from his hospital bed. There was a little metal box hidden away in our closet I was to open after his death. Reluctantly I turned the key in the small lock, took out the papers, and began to read. Don had kept a journal of his thoughts over the past three years, expressing his feelings about his death. He had been grieving too, far more than I knew, shedding tears before the Lord, though never before me or the children. He was losing his family; for him, it was as though we were the ones dying. At the bottom of the box was a personal letter to me expressing his love and prayers for my future.

In the last sentence he wrote: "I'm trusting the Lord to bring another man into your life to give you the love you deserve."

The thought of Don praying for my future husband brought fresh tears. Only a truly great, loving, and unselfish man would have prayed that way.

I knew I could never settle for less than I had had with Don, but I also knew God wasn't in the business of giving second best. Eventually I did begin asking God to send into my life a godly man of His choosing. Then I became more specific.

"Lord," I said, "I want to marry in Your will, but please might he be a widower about my own age. And it would greatly simplify matters if he didn't have children of his own."

I knew my three children had been through such a bad time adapting without their own father that they didn't need the added complication of other children in the home. For me, this prayer seemed right.

One day nearly a year after Don's death I received a letter from friends asking if I would come visit them. I really needed a brief vacation, so I quickly accepted. It was summer, and the children could stay with their grandparents.

While I was visiting them, my friends gave a small dinner for me and that night introduced me to tall, good-looking Jim Leonard. I smiled inwardly. My friends everywhere knew "just the perfect man for you."

But this time they were right. After dinner Jim and I sat and talked like old friends.

Jim had been widowed for over a year, and he and his wife had been childless. He invited me to dinner the next evening, and we were both able to talk out our feelings of loss and loneliness.

Jim courted me by mail, by long-distance telephone calls, and by flying visits to my home. We knew, but didn't admit it until much later, that we had fallen in love that first night. When Jim pulled me close and asked me to marry him, tears glistened in my eyes. The feel of a man's strong arms, the touch of love kindling one heart to another awakened my slumbering heart. I whispered "yes."

A nagging doubt persisted that the children might be less than enthused about a move to a small town, and I was right. They didn't want to leave their home and friends, and what should have been a happy time became troubled.

It took continual prayer and lots of loving on our part to convince them that Jim was not an intruder, but someone who loved us and would be part of our family."

When we *were* once again a complete, loving family, I breathed a sigh of relief. I wanted to get on with living, especially closing the door forever on death.

But that's one door that always stands open; the only uncertainty is when we are to go through it. My father and mother, whom I loved dearly and who had been so supportive of me during Don's illness, died within two years of each other. And then I understood why the Lord had given me Jim so quickly.

I remember thinking after my parents died, "I'm glad this life isn't all there is or it would be a mockery, just living, loving, and losing."

"There are some ways to prepare for widowhood, perhaps not emotionally, but practically," Kathy Melton Leonard said. "That is not to say we should live in daily dread that we *will* lose our husbands, but we should at some point face the fact that we *might*. Most important of all we must be assured that God is who He says He is, *The Lord who provides" (Gen. 22:14)*.

Kathy was given time to prepare for her loss, although this didn't lessen her mourning. However it doesn't always happen that way. Often, happily married young women—are suddenly single, plunged into widowhood in an instant, their plans and lives shattered. One of these women is Marilyn O'Neal.

## Marilyn

On a cool September morning Marilyn O'Neal looked out the kitchen window across acres and acres of Iowa farmland nearly ready for harvesting and smiled with contentment.

She watched her husband Kevin perched high on the combine and next to him in his favorite place their two-year-old Bobby, fair hair gleaming in the morning sunlight, his face aglow with the delight of sitting way up high with daddy working in the fields.

It was time to harvest soybeans, and Kevin was

checking out the combine to be sure it was ready for the tremendous task ahead of them. Marilyn turned back to her chores in the house, a smile playing about her lips. As much as Kevin loved the farm, she knew his heart was really down in the yard where his new motorcycle stood, bright red with shiny chrome. Farming was first because that could not wait, but Marilyn sensed Kevin was hurrying through his chores in time to take a ride across the roads around their country town.

The repairs on the combine were done before lunch and a smiling Kevin was at the door. Kevin's grin had disarmed her from the first moment she saw him years before at a high school football game. His blond, tousled hair was as endearing today as it had been thirteen years before when they stood at the altar pledging their vows.

What more could she ask for? Kevin, her love; eleven-year-old Debby, the daughter she cherished; and now two-year-old Bobby, his daddy's joyful pride.

Marilyn had been raised in this small farming community, hardly traveling beyond its borders, and though she read extensively, journeying to distant places in her imagination, she was content to be what she was: Kevin O'Neal's wife.

Now she turned, knowing what he would say: "I'm taking the bike out for a spin. We won't have many more nice days, and after we begin combining I won't have the time." He grinned again knowing Marilyn would understand his need for racing the bike along narrow dirt roads, the wind freeing him from the world of farming, soybeans, and harvesting.

"Your right, hon." Marilyn blew a kiss. "I'll keep an eye on things here while you're gone."

Kevin answered with a blown-back kiss, their private

gesture of love often thrown across acres of land, a symbol of "I'm right there with you."

Marilyn and Bobby held hands as they watched the roaring motorcycle take off down the long dirt driveway and turn onto the highway in front of their farmhouse. She was certain Kevin wouldn't be home until the sun glowed in its magnificient sunset and disappeared. Dinner would have to be late tonight.

At six o'clock she loaded Debby and the neighborhood children into her blue station wagon to drive them to choir. She wondered once more why rehearsal had to be at this inconvenient hour.

It was nearly dark at six-fifty when she drove back to the church to pick up the children. A tiny frown of concern creased her brow for it was past sunset and Kevin should have come home by now. Still, he had many friends in town; he may have met someone, got to talking, and let the time slip by.

On the highway ahead Marilyn saw the flashing lights of county patrol cars. Probably a minor accident. And in a flurry of irritation at the hold up it would cause, she quickly made a detour to the church parking lot, scurried the children into the wagon, and drove home a back way to avoid the accident scene. As she made the turn into their long driveway, Marilyn looked for the red motorcycle to be parked in its usual place. She was sure Kevin would be anxiously awaiting her return home to start dinner. Her heart sank. There was no bike and the house was dark.

Debby and Bobby were distracting her with their chatter, and suddenly she noticed in the rear-view mirror that a car was coming up fast behind them. It was the mailman's car and in the front seat with him sat the fire chief. They followed her up to the house and when she got out of the driver's seat and looked at their faces she knew that the accident she had so carefully avoided must have involved Kevin.

"Marilyn," the mailman, who often stopped by for a morning cup of coffee and chit-chat, said, "it's Kevin. Get in our car." She looked anxiously at the children, but the two men gently lead them along. "We'll drop the children at the neighbor's house."

Her stunned mind could only obey. They stopped to leave the children with the neighbor and then raced the fourteen miles to the town's small hospital.

"How badly is he hurt?" her voice sounded distant to her ears, but there was only an ominous silence from the men on either side of her. She began to babble nervously, not waiting for an answer. "He's had a cold, a bad cough. If he has chest injuries it will only complicate his cough. Oh, I hope it's not his chest."

Silence!

"Who will do the field work with soybeans coming in and corn harvesting if Kevin is badly hurt? We have one hundred sixty sows ready to have young any time."

More silence! The chief squeezed her hand, and she thought briefly how kind it was of him to be so concerned.

The small hospital came into view, and when they stopped, Marilyn jumped from the car. She knew the ambulance driver well, but when she looked at him he turned away, busying himself with his vehicle. Kevin must be seriously hurt, she thought, racing for the door to emergency.

Several doctors and nurses were standing together in the hall and didn't see Marilyn approaching. She stopped abruptly when a nurse asked, "Is there any next of kin here?"

178

*Next of kin?* Marilyn's heart began to hammer wildly. There in the nurse's hand was Kevin's wallet, the brown wallet she had given him last Christmas.

She reached for it numbly, her hands clammy. Wouldn't anybody speak to her? Did she have to think the most horrible thought? Was Kevin dead?

Surely, at any minute Kevin would walk through those doors, put his arms around her, and hold her trembling body. *Kevin! Kevin, don't leave me!*

As the panic flared, a door swung open and their family doctor, a lifelong friend, walked to her side, put his arm around her, and lead her to a chapel down the hall.

"Then . . . then Kevin's dead?" she stated the words so he would have to confirm her worst fears. He nodded slightly, sitting down with her in the cool of the small sanctuary.

"Widow," she was thinking. "I'm a widow." But she must have said the words aloud. Dr. Farraday nodded gravely.

"I want to go home," she said firmly. "I want to be with the children." The only ties she had with Kevin now were her precious Debby and Bobby. She arose resolutely, tears still refusing to come. Dr. Farraday drove her home, back down the long dirt highway, past the green acres of land ready to be harvested, along their beloved farmland. The sight of the combine waiting in the driveway tore at her bruised heart.

The kind doctor had stopped for the children, and now she wondered how she could tell her small son that he would never see his daddy again; that that morning on top of the combine had been his last minutes with his adored father. Debby was crying softly, and Marilyn took her hand.

The small farming community became like family to

Marilyn and her children. It was almost as though they had lost a son. Kevin had grown up in their midst; he was loved and respected as a young farmer. They rallied around pouring out love, bringing food, and taking over chores that could not be ignored, not even for death.

The friends who were most comforting were the ones with outstretched arms who let her grieve, mourn, and cry out without restraint, understanding that her grief was great and that it was natural for her to weep from the center of her being.

The funeral service was packed with family and friends. When the minister quoted the words of Jesus, "Because I live you shall live also," Marilyn wondered if it were true. She wasn't sure that was a promise Kevin could claim. As far as she knew, he had never made a personal decision to follow Jesus Christ, to accept Him as Savior and Lord, and the emptiness of not knowing became a bitter cross she would bear forever.

A few years before she had surrendered her own life to the Lord. Kevin never understood why she had changed, though she told him over and over that it was the Lord who had given her a new life, a different attitude, taken away old habits that were no longer right for the new Marilyn.

It seemed a price Kevin would not pay.

"But it's not giving up anything, Kev," she had said. "It's getting the very best God has . . . His Son bringing salvation, forgiveness, eternal life."

But Kevin was young. Maybe someday, he had said, smiling patronizingly, and patting her hand.

That day had never come for him.

After the flowers were gone and family and friends had to return to their own homes and chores, Marilyn lost her will to step one foot outside her door. Her home became a haven where she could sit and weep and mourn her loss.

If only . . . if only she knew that Kevin had made his peace with God. He had chosen to reject God's gift of eternal life . . . unless . . . unless in that final moment. . . . Had Kevin met God there as he lay dying by his motorbike? It was a tiny hope Marilyn would cling to, but she could never really know. In the week after the funeral she thought that she would never really live again or care what happened to the farm. The world could whirl around without her, for the center of her life had been ripped away.

One morning Marilyn awakened and heard the sound of the roosters in the barnyard. Why hadn't she heard them last week? Had her ears been deafened with shock? There were six hundred acres to be farmed; neighbors and friends couldn't help forever. She who had so loved being a farmer's wife must now be the farmer.

The September morning was overcast, unlike the morning two weeks before when Kevin had stuck his head around the door and told her he was taking the bike for a spin, blowing her a last kiss.

Decisions had to be made. She was the sole owner of six hundred acres ready to be harvested. She had two children depending on her for love and security. She called her family and the farmhands together, and they sat at the kitchen table to map out future plans.

"Kevin isn't here to do the work," Marilyn said from her place at the head, "but we must do things as he would have done them." She began to give orders, organizing the day's work. She who had stayed in the kitchen baking bread, canning bushels of fruit was running the farm with an inner strength and wisdom she didn't know she possessed.

She wondered how she could be so sure that things should be done a certain way, but one day she found the answer in the Psalms. "I will instruct you and teach you in the way you should go; I will counsel you and watch over you" (Ps. 32:8). She had read that verse many times before but had never related it to mundane things like how much feed to order, how many farmhands to hire; now she was certain that at this point that was exactly what it meant for her. Her heart lifted. What a promise to keep beside her! *God* was instructing and teaching and counseling her, Marilyn O'Neal, in every detail of farming. Each morning she claimed that promise, and each night she fell into bed exhausted but exhilarated at what had been accomplished.

She sat long hours in attorneys' offices learning to understand their particular language, trying to get her affairs in order, wondering why she hadn't paid more attention when Kevin was working on the books and explaining about insurance and such. But there had seemed no need at the time. Night after night she worked on papers, filing, posting figures in small columns, until one night she pushed them aside and sank into Kevin's easy chair and let tears flow without bothering to wipe them away. She rubbed the leather chair as though she could somehow touch Kevin.

"Oh, Kev," she sobbed, "why did you leave me?" She wept long into the dark night, her suffering reaching a peak she hoped would never be as intense again.

"God," she cried, "You have to be the center of my life now. Kev is gone. I have no one else." *If only His arms could be around me the way Kevin's were,* she thought wearily, and words slipped into her mind, words she couldn't quite remember—something about "everlasting arms." She would look it up someday when she had the will to think clearly.

It was work that was her greatest therapy: rising at five o'clock and working until the last wagon of shelled corn was unloaded late at night.

Debby grew up overnight—cooking, babysitting for Bobby, taking telephone messages—and Marilyn blessed God over and over for giving her such a responsible child.

Finally the harvest was over, and winter began its relentless snowstorms and blizzards, a time of restlessness for the young widow. During past winters Kevin had lit the fireplace on snowy nights and they had sat together holding hands, letting the snow fly where it would; they were content to be snowed in together.

Now she was alone after the children slept. She began quieting her loneliness with the comforting Psalms, outlining verses that spoke to her needs, studying long into the wintry night.

It seemed impossible to face Christmas without Kevin. She shopped quickly without enthusiasm, decorating the tree she had bought this year, unable and unwilling to relive the memory of past Christmases when they had trudged through the snow to find "the perfect tree" to chop down. Her parents came to spend the holidays, and for that she was grateful.

"When will the hurt go away, mom?" she cried on Christmas Eve after the gifts were opened and the children were in bed, their new toys neatly stacked under the tree.

"You've lost part of yourself, Marilyn, honey," her mother said, gently stroking her daughter's hair.

"Just cry, honey. It's okay. Just cry." And she hummed a song she had sung when Marilyn was a baby, cradling her.

Spring flowered in, an unusually lovely one, and Marilyn worked harder than ever to keep the farm going, hiring more farmhands. They sowed bountifully that year, and once more Marilyn was clearly guided and instructed on every decision she had to make.

Marilyn O'Neal, always loved in the community, became a person to point to with pride. "She did it all herself," the neighboring farmers would say, "that plucky little girl. Never thought she had it in her, but she rose up like a commander and did what had to be done."

But Marilyn knew otherwise. She had not done it "all herself." One night in her Bible study she found a verse that lifted her stricken heart. A light went on in her soul that has never dimmed.

> For I know the plans I have for you, says the Lord.
> They are plans for good and not for evil, to give you
> a future and a hope. In those days when you pray, I will
> listen. You will find me when you seek me, if you look for
> me in earnest" (Jer. 29:11–13 LB).

If you ever have the pleasure of meeting Marilyn, she will tell you that she found that verse about God's "everlasting arms" and that it became her rock and strength. She may smile in the soft way she has and paraphrase it like this:

"The eternal God has been, is, and forever will be my refuge, and underneath me, Marilyn O'Neal, are His everlasting arms."

Beyond
Heartache

# Beyond Heartache

As I mentioned in the preface, every story in this book is true. And there are many heartaches and sorrows of life we have not even touched on: war, poverty, injustice, racial prejudice, abused and neglected children, suicide, loneliness, and on and on.

Surrounded by all of this, sooner or later we ask the question: Why heartache? Why suffering?

And many times our questions remain unanswered, for the ways of God are beyond our understanding. Yet in the Bible He has given us a glimmer of insight into some of the "whys."

We live in an imperfect world, the consequence of rebellion in Eden.

Satan is active in human lives, attempting to destroy faith and trust in a loving heavenly Father as he tried to do in the life of Job.

Suffering in one form or another *will* come to those who live a godly life (2 Tim. 3:12).

We may be enticed and carried away by our own lust, perhaps reaping the most terrible heartache of all: the harvest of our own rebellion and disobedience toward God (James 1:14, 15).

Or, pain, suffering, and death may be allowed so that God might receive the greater glory (John 9:3).

But there *is* a life that produces joy in spite of heartache and faith in the midst of trials. It is the Christian life. This life promises something beyond heartache, beyond grief, beyond disappointment, beyond life's darkest valley, and that is *hope*. Hope is: reliance on the absolute certainty that "In all things God works for the good of those who love him (Rom. 8:28), and total faith in the ultimate assurance that this life is not all there is, "For this world is not our home; we are looking forward to our everlasting home in heaven" (Heb. 13:14 LB). We can rely on the unshakable promise that "God is our refuge and strength, an ever present help in trouble" (Ps. 46:1).

During rough times of personal heartache, I often wondered where the unbeliever took his or her deepest grief and intolerable burdens. Now I know in part! Some search for temporary release in affairs, divorce, alcohol, drugs, rebellion, or even in so-called religion. And their heartache is compounded. Others may exist on a seething anger, fueling their lives with the flames of bitterness. Unwilling to *let go* of their lost loved ones, they refuse to relinquish their hold on past memories and thus suffer the consequences of a lifetime of sorrow.

But even though one is a recipient of this new life in

Christ, he or she is not guaranteed a future free from troubles, for Christians are Satan's prime target. At times, God intervenes miraculously, delivering His children from trials. More often He does not. But always He offers His power, presence, and peace as we go through deep valleys.

His promise is the same today as it was centuries ago when the apostle Paul beseeched the Lord for deliverance from his "thorn in the flesh."

"No," God answered, "but I am with you; that is all you need" (2 Cor. 12:9 LB).

Paul also commands us to bear one another's burdens. "When others are troubled, needing our sympathy and encouragement, we can pass on to them this same help and comfort God has given us. You can be sure that the more we undergo sufferings for Christ, the more he will shower us with his comfort and encouragement. . . . But in our trouble God had comforted us—and this, too, to help you: to show you from our personal experience how God will tenderly comfort you when you undergo these same sufferings. *He will give you the strength to endure"* (2 Cor. 1:4-7 LB).

"Those who hope in the Lord will renew their strength. They will soar on wings like eagles; they will run and not grow weary, they will walk and not be faint" (Isa. 40:31).

And that is the difference! *Hope in the Lord!* Not hoping that the wayward husband will return, not hoping for the rebellious child to change his ways, not hoping for circumstances to change and the problem to be resolved, but *hoping in the Lord.* The beautiful picture of a eagle soaring high above the circumstances is the picture God gives of the trusting, hoping heart.

This new life beyond heartache begins at the foot of the cross, the only bridge between sinful humanity and a holy

God, the only place of forgiveness, mercy, fulfillment, peace, and freedom. But we do not come to Jesus Christ to relieve heartache or to receive inspiration or to ease a troubled conscious. *We come because we are sinners in desperate need of a Savior; we come because it is a matter of life or death.*

Jesus Christ left a legacy for His followers, one the world can never contest: a bequest of *His* love, *His* joy, and *His* peace. And because it is *His*, it is perfect and lasting.

God has promised that there will not be peace in this world until Jesus the Prince of Peace returns. However, He did promise peace to each heart that would surrender to Him: peace that nothing can disturb, peace through trials, peace through heartache, peace through tears.

Millions can say, "It is true" to God's own words spoken centuries ago:

> *When you go through deep waters and great trouble, I will be with you. When you go through rivers of difficulty, you will not drown! When you walk through the fire of oppression, you will not be burned up— the flames will not consume you* (Isa. 43:2 LB, *italics mine*).

The ultimate . . . the final hope? *There's a new world coming!* A time and place for all who believe, for all who are under His mercy and grace. A final place *beyond all heartache*, forever and ever.

Listen:

> *Then I saw a new earth and a new sky; for the present earth and sky had disappeared. And I, John, saw the Holy City, the new Jerusalem, coming down from God out of heaven. It was a glorious sight, beautiful as a bride at her wedding.*

*I heard a loud shout from the throne saying, "Look, the home of God is now among men, and he will live with them and they will be his people; yes, God himself will be among them. He will wipe away all tears from their eyes, and there shall be no more death, nor sorrow, nor crying, nor pain. All of that has gone forever" (Rev. 21:1–4 LB).*